WENTWORTH-DOUGLASS HOSPITAL

A Place of Healing

A History of Wentworth-Douglass Hospital

by Noreen A. Biehl

Printed in the United States of America

First Printing, 2016

ISBN 978-0-9977547-0-4

Contact Publisher:
Wentworth-Douglass Hospital
789 Central Avenue
Dover, NH 03820
www.wdhospital.com

Designed by William C. Wolff
www.williamwolff.com

Printed by R.C. Brayshaw & Company
www.rcbrayshaw.com

Photos courtesy of Wentworth-Douglass Hospital, except where noted.

Author's Note

My first memory of Wentworth-Douglass Hospital was probably distorted, seen through the eyes of a worried mother concerned about her seven-year old bike crasher fidgeting next to his younger sister in the busy ER waiting room almost 40 years ago. I remember a room filled with anxious people, cigarette smoke, and the sounds of coins clicking as they dropped into nearby vending machines. A single employee asked personal questions as each patient or parent queued up, writing in a large log book. Confidentiality and seating were limited. Dr. Peter Bradley, a sandy-haired man who always looked a little wrinkled, somewhat sleepy, and blissfully calm, ignored the little biker's squirms and deftly stitched him up.

A decade passed before I returned. Neither a patient nor a parent of a patient, this time I came for a job. As a former reporter with the very newspaper that covered the hospital since it was founded, I met the bare essentials to work in PR. Director Mary Perry hired me to be her assistant. Before my first day on the job, she was hospitalized for an undisclosed and, sadly, terminal illness. The Hospital Administrator William C. Richwagen took charge of me, no doubt with some reluctance. From that day on I always reported to the CEO, a fate that changed my life in many ways. I learned a lot about hospitals, finance, caring and sharing in the lives of incredible people - even people I never knew.

My first office was a narrow, wood-paneled room on the second floor of the Rollins building that was once home to nursing students. I shared the space with bookcases of Wentworth-Douglass Hospital's historical records. Heavy scrapbooks held cracked plastic pages of old news clippings next to battered boxes of old photos, handwritten documents, and collections of the city's annual reports dating from the early 1900s. This is where I began my journey back to the early 20th century to discover a remarkable era when the country was run by a swashbuckling president. Captains of industry gave generously to good causes and hospitals transitioned from infirmaries providing custodial care to institutions of science and technology where X-rays, labs, aseptic techniques, and skilled caregivers turned them into places of healing.

This history covers the hospital's 110 years, gleaned from annual reports, news stories, on-line sources, hospital publications, remembrances, and interviews. The people and events are limited to recorded information and the voices of key representatives of the hospital over time - the CEOs, Board members, past and current physicians, administrative staff. It is still only a glimpse at the past. I wished I could have included the names and stories of everyone connected to the hospital - thousands of exceptional people who took care of a growing community and made Wentworth-Douglass Hospital a very special place.

Table of Contents

Prologue – December 13, 2012

The subtly patterned carpet muffled his steps as he walked the long, curved hallways in the new Garrison Wing. Glass sconces lit the way, marking the entrances to patient rooms quietly waiting for future guests. The late afternoon sun streamed through the multi-paned windows facing Central Avenue, painting each room with rectangles of warm light on this cool December day. This was Greg Walker's last chance to take a solo tour in a building he had envisioned years ago, soon after he became President & CEO of Wentworth-Douglass Hospital.

More than a decade had passed since the last physical vestige of the hospital's past, the old Rollins Nurses Home, crumbled under the weight of a wrecking ball. Greg remembered the day he decided to take it down; he knew it would not

go unnoticed and might generate a few irate Letters to the Editor or a front page story as the local paper liked to do. It didn't matter that the building had already crumbled under the weight of time, neglect, and loss of purpose; for some fervent preservationists, the spirits of 1920s nursing students, in crisp white aprons, still survived as they gathered in the ornate living room for afternoon tea and capping ceremonies.

Today was the beginning of a new era; a shift from old, crowded nursing units where carts rattled down narrow, vinyl-tiled hallways and patients shared small rooms and their most personal health issues with strangers. Greg knew patients, families, and their caregivers would relish the new spaces. He wanted the rooms to feel as warm as a patient's home. He had often visited the building during construction, watching cranes lift walls of brick, easing them effortlessly into place. The flickering flat screen TVs reminded him of the day he watched skilled electricians thread miles of wires and computer cables along ceiling joists, down steel studs, and into switch plates. Even though he was anxious for the building to open, he would miss seeing talented craftsmen install tile, lay carpet, and turn the lights on. The carpenters and painters were gone for now, at least until the nicks and cracks that came with time would need repair.

Greg's tour began on the top floor, "4 G" as it would be known in just a few weeks. After moving past the floor's 32 patient rooms, he stepped down the back stairway to 3G, a floor almost identical to the one above with a dedicated rehab center tucked into its mid-section. He knew the room's unique feature, a half of a car, donated by Seacoast Orthopedics and Sports Medicine, would delight patients as they began their therapy and learned how to get in and out of their rides again. He purposely took the elevator down to the second floor to experience, as the doors opened, the revealing of an immense landscape crafted in glass, marking the entry to the Women & Children's Center. The gleaming scene de-

picted a family playing in a field of trees on an early autumn day; a collage of yellows, greens, and oranges against a bright blue background. He wanted everything about this center to be welcoming - a place to celebrate the joy of birth and kids getting better.

Another elevator ride to the first floor opened into the Garrison Wing Conference Center. The quiet ended as he entered

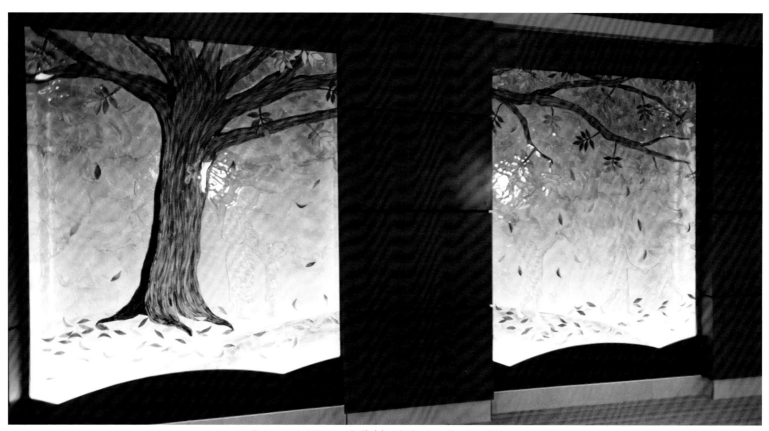

Entrance to Women & Children's Center, Garrison Wing.

this floor. The entire center was poised for the day's dedication event, decked out with holiday trees dressed in tiny lights, white poinsettias, and bronze ribbons. The back of the conference center lobby featured a wall of backlit beacon logos cut out of a cherry wood panel. Its four auditoriums were open to their full size, greeting techs testing microphones and video equipment while staff set up rows of chairs. The podium waited for the evening to begin.

Greg's speech, in bold type, was folded in the inside pocket of his dark suit. He had worked on it for many days. His comments were heartfelt but, he admitted, probably similar to those who had gone before him, each crafting their own descriptions of a "modern" hospital. Time always took its toll until the next modernization took place or the next CEO came in. Greg hoped Wentworth-Douglass would continue as one of the finest hospitals in the region for decades to come. He would do his best to make it happen. He made one more stop as he exited the Garrison Wing to look outside at the Healing Garden. A subtle breeze caressed the tall wind sculpture, turning it gently in the frosty air against a deepening grey sky, hinting at possible snow. In this same spot, so many years ago, student nurses gathered for afternoon tea.

August 30, 1906
Grace tucked a stray hair into the neat swirl at the back of her head, trying not to look too severe but also trying to exude the traits she so admired and knew others expected; competence, orderliness, perfection. Her long strand of pearls seemed perfect - not too elaborate, yet elegant in an understated way. She stopped momentarily to look out the window of her suite on the first floor of the Administration Building as the sun moved higher in the sky defining the edges of the long stone wall and broad steps that led from Central Avenue to the entrance of the Wentworth Hospital.

After months of construction, mounds of dirt and brick dust, this stately hospital at the top of Garrison Hill was about to open its doors to Dover and its citizens. But it was Grace's hospital as much as it was the city's. Her training at Maine General Hospital, followed by caring for soldiers suffering from typhoid at a Philadelphia hospital, and managing Portland's St. Barnabas Hospital, had duly impressed the new Wentworth Hospital Board of Trustees when they offered her the superintendent position. She would care for the hospital with all her nurse's discipline, knowledge, and pride. Dedication ceremonies were set to begin at 2:30 p.m. She walked one final, quiet time through its three main structures and five corridors connecting six, small buildings. There was no doubt about the identity of the hospital's namesake once visitors entered the reception hall on the main floor of the Administration Building. A life-size oil portrait of its benefactor, Arioch Wentworth, edged in a thick gold frame, graced the lobby. Painted in his mature years, he appeared vigorous and professorial in his black suit and waistcoat stretched over his ample frame.

Beyond the entry, just past a broad staircase was the Trustees Room, furnished by the daughters of Dr. Levi Hill, one of Dover's leading physicians and honored citizens. Grace admired the woodwork in white-stained North Carolina pine and the dark green walls. There were eight chairs, a sofa, and a table, all solid mahogany, rich in color, massive and colonial in style. It was a picture of rich, quiet harmony. Grace continued her inspection as the early afternoon sun seeped through the octagonal walls of windows facing Central Avenue in each of the male and female pavilions. The ten beds in each of the wards were dressed in starched, white linens ready for their first patients. The sunny balconies surrounding the pavilions would soon bring welcome breezes to recovering patients over the remaining summer days and each ward's fireplace would chase the chill from a blustery, winter day.

North of the female pavilion was the operating pavilion. Lighted by a skylight, it contained preparation and etherizing rooms, sanitary flooring, and enameled walls. Grace moved on to the Nurses Hall, across from the male pavilion, lightly touching the medical books and training documents lining the shelves in its library. Her hand settled on the one she had authored, the *Training School for Nurses Manual*. This slim handbook was thorough, perhaps strict in some ways, but it was the essential guide for the young women seeking to be nurses in her hospital. The proper training of student nurses was more important to Grace than mahogany furniture and massive portraits of men long gone. She knew the future of this institution depended on many factors including the expertise of its physicians, the quality of its equipment and medicines and, dear to her heart, the vital role nurses played in caring for the sick.

Over two thousand men, women, and children toured the hospital on that warm, summer day. Their horse drawn carriages clattered up the avenue, occupants dressed in their finest attire; the women wore long billowy skirts, lace trimmed blouses, and wide brimmed hats; the men came in three piece suits, stiff collared shirts, and straw boaters. Curious visitors strolled over the waxed and highly polished white maple floors as they toured the new Wentworth Hospital.

Grace watched the keynote speaker and well-known orator, Col. Daniel Hall, as he strode up to the dais, straightened his elegant black suit, stroked his well-groomed mustache as if it might be in the way, and, took a deep breath to deliver his address. She knew he had a reputation for being long-winded and he certainly didn't disappoint. His lengthy tribute to the hospital's benefactor was filled with an assortment of accolades, aspirations, and occasional references to a caring deity. She noticed the crowd of citizens fidgeting in straight-backed chairs as they listened to Col. Hall praise Arioch Wentworth. She was impressed with Wentworth's life story, laboring on his father's farm in Somersworth "till he nearly attained his majority" and working for his passage on a "gundalow laden with brick" as he headed to Boston where he flourished in the soap-stone and marble businesses. She thought Hall sounded a bit like a preacher at times, praising Wentworth's accomplishments saying, "he couldn't help making money," and noting he was "believed to be the largest real estate owner in Boston and the tax lists there for many years before his death bore witness to how extensively God helps those who help themselves."

When he ended his speech by saying, "the sciences of medicine and surgery, and public charity, are all in the making and still in the gristle, and he who lives 50 years, as some of you will, will see this institution a much larger one than we launch or contemplate today," Grace was reminded again of her duty to sustain this gift through the inevitable good times and bad times ahead.

Foster's Daily Democrat covered the dedicatory exercises on the front page of their August 30, 1906 edition, highlighting the "good attendance and interesting program ably addressed by Col. Daniel Hall" along with other news of the world. Grace approved of the front page story that chose not to run the full text of Col. Hall's commentary. She did notice other news stories that day including a piece on equal rights denied to women in Melbourne, Australia. She believed in the equality of men and women and hoped to see a day when women got the right to vote.

Part 1: The Early Years (1906-1969)

Dover, N.H., Wentworth Hospital.

Chapter 1: The Early 20ᵗʰ Century, A City Builds a Hospital

The first decades of the 1900s saw remarkable inventions, the development of sulfa antimicrobials and penicillin, the tragedies of a world war, and a deadly flu epidemic. Two unsinkable ships, the Titanic and the Lusitania met their demise in cold Atlantic seas and the Wright Brothers took flight at Kitty Hawk. In 1906, the year the Wentworth Hospital opened, 45 United States came together with aspirations of better days after surviving the tragic losses of a civil war and reconstruction struggles. Both the benefits and challenges of rapid industrialization fueled inventive minds and swelled the ranks of immigrants to work in textile mills, labor in factories, and too often, die from unsafe conditions or pernicious diseases. President Teddy Roosevelt's progressive policies suggested government needed to consider adopting some form of health insurance but another century would pass before legislation succeeded. Life expectancy hovered at 48 years, not due to a lack of nonagenarians but to the staggering death rate of infants and children from birthing mishaps and infectious diseases.

Arioch Wentworth

The early 20ᵗʰ century in Dover, New Hampshire began with a city recovering from a tragic flood that severely diminished its shipping industry even as its cotton and woolen mills kept spinning. The City Councils were intent on rebuilding and even flourishing as they reaped the benefits of affluent industrialists such as Arioch Wentworth and Andrew Carnegie. In 1904, the councils accepted Wentworth's legacy gift and purchased a three acre Central Avenue lot on Garrison Hill from Harrison Haley for $3,000. They believed the land to be "the best of all those offered" due to its "commanding location, high and dry, with a porous soil, easily drained." It was "convenient to the electric and steam railways" and accessible to "all the compact parts of the city, yet not so closely surrounded by dwellings as to make it objectionable to any neighborhood."

Mayor G. J. Foster's 1906 valedictory address praised the new high school, completed in 1905 as "second to none in the state" and urged citizens to visit the new Carnegie-funded library, built next to and in the same year as the high school.

A "perusal" of the new books and periodicals in the library, he wrote, "will repay even the most obtuse mind." Mayor Foster's commentary included a reference to the opening of the Wentworth Hospital, the appointment of a Board of Trustees entrusted with the Wentworth legacy of $100,000 to construct a hospital in Dover, and the text of the lengthy dedication speeches. Board Chairman John Kivel's introductory remarks described the Wentworth Hospital as "a thoroughly equipped and well appointed modern hospital" and a "refuge for the sick and afflicted" regardless "of race, creed, or purse." After its first few months of operation, Mayor Foster congratulated the hospital for exceeding anticipated revenue. He surmised the city might be called upon to "to pay a much less sum" to care for those unable to pay. All hopes were dashed within a few years when the number of "wholly free" patients rose to over twenty percent, and costs to care grew beyond expectations.

The Wentworth Hospital by-laws contained the standard terms of office sections with a rather politically correct admonition that "at no time shall all members of said board be of the same political party." Remaining sections were tightly focused on costs and limiting expenses where possible. In an era without antibiotics and little ability to cure disease, the hospital's Board determined "incurable patients" were not to be admitted, unless, "in the opinion of the Superintendent, there are indications that such patient might be relieved." Later reports reveal this rule to be consistently violated in order to provide comfort for dying patients. Free patients, who were able, were required to "render light service" and "to do so when requested by the Superintendent."

While the names of patients were not included in reports, their occupations, ability to pay, and place of birth were carefully annotated. Of the 75 patients admitted during its first year, one was a sea captain along with some farmers, shoemakers, saloon keepers, and housewives. Most were born in the US or immigrated from Ireland, Scotland, England and Canada, but a few came from faraway locations including Syria, Turkey, Italy, Germany and Russia. Charges ranged from $1.50 in a ward to $3.50 per day for one of eight private rooms. Physician charges were independent of hospital fees.

Chapter 2: Grace Haskell takes charge

As Grace Haskell wrapped the reins of a fledgling hospital around her caring hands, she began a 30-year journey as its leader in chief. In her first report to the city, she noted, the domestic department was "running smoothly" despite "frequent changes in the working force." Evidence still exists of the employment fluctuations in a small, tattered journal that bears a handwritten label, "Record for Help, August 1, 1906 to May 31, 1918". Using an ink pen that may have been one of the new Parker fountain pens, Grace created simple, one page entries for each employee during that period, listing date of hire, date of departure, and reason for leaving. The very first entry in this frayed document lists the name of a cook, hired on August 1, 1906 and discharged on August 31, 1906. The reason she noted, "Was No Cook." In another section she drew four columns headed by date, name, position, and amount paid monthly. Janitor Eugene Palmer was the highest paid of nine listed in the hospital's first year at $50 per month, followed by the cook at $30, and the laundress at $25.

Nurses were paid separately as defined in Grace's training manual. "After a probationary period has expired, ten dollars a month will be paid for the first year; twelve dollars a month for the second year; and fourteen dollars per month for the remainder of the course. This is for personal expenses, and is not to be considered as remuneration for services. The training is a full equivalent for time rendered."

Superintendent Grace P. Haskell, RN

Oct. 1916

Eugene Palmer	Janitor	50.00
Julia Randal	cook	30.00
Mathi Brown	Waitress	14.00
Mary Callahan	Laundress	25.00
Eda Winslow	N. maid	14.00
	N.	14.00

Sat. Oct. 6. 1906

In her manual, Grace was particularly focused on an exacting dress code and personal hygiene. "Applicants should bring the following articles: three gingham or calico dresses, eight aprons of bleached cotton, two yards wide meeting in back, band two inches wide with two buttons and button-holes, hem four inches deep and two inches from the bottom of the dress; two bags for soiled clothes, one pair of scissors, a pin ball, and a napkin ring; a good supply of plain under clothing - every article marked with the owner's name. Twenty-four pieces are allowed for laundry each week. Noiseless boots must be worn, and garments suitable for out-of-door wear in stormy weather must be brought. The teeth are to be in order."

Over the next ten years, the hospital purchased additional property from the Haley farm for $5,700, later sold back (1921) to Rollinsford, and even later (1978) bought back. Grace's reports thanked donors who gave fruit, pickles, magazines, and records for the Victor Talking machine. A donated flag and staff, she noted, were raised for the first time on Christmas Day in 1914. Staffing difficulties were often mentioned. Domestic staff were hard to keep when "women can obtain employment in the mills or factories." She was concerned about increasing drug prices and she pleaded, unsuccessfully, for the city to consider constructing an isolation building when a measles epidemic broke out in 1916. A year later, while war raged in Europe, Grace's report highlighted a hospital doing its part and living with less. She wrote that the supply of many articles was not equal to the demand. The hospital had "Hooverized" on more lines than food and the call of the country for all kinds of supplies was heeded as a patriotic duty. The hospital joined the canning campaign and canned "over 700 jars of fruit and tomatoes besides much jelly." Two graduate nurses responded to the call for overseas duty as part of a Red Cross Unit and the need for nurses grew more imperative as the "cruel war" continued.

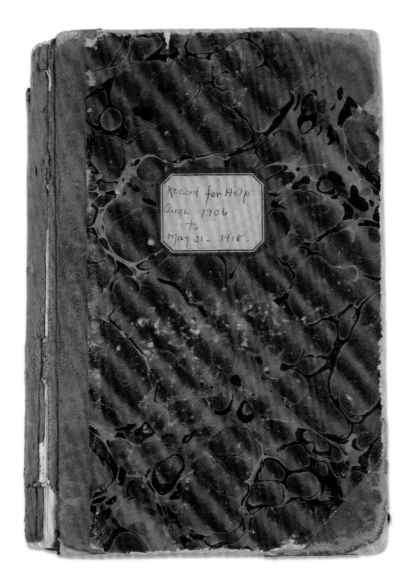

The World War ended in November 1918. While casualties were high, the Spanish Flu epidemic was even deadlier that year, estimated to have killed more US soldiers than the bitter battle. The prevalence of influenza not only taxed the "capacity of the hospital, but the physical strength of the entire force of the institution." Grace reported, "of the 21 nurses on staff, 18 developed influenza." She wrote, "Those of us who saw it through from the beginning have nightmare memories that time can never wholly efface. No soldier could display greater bravery than our pupil nurses."

The following year brought welcome news when the Hon. Edward W. Rollins, of Three Rivers Farm, donated $25,000 for the purpose of erecting a nurses home as a memorial to the late Gladys A. Rollins - the beloved wife of his son, Ashton Rollins. The fund was later increased to $81,000 to cover the full cost of construction. In gratitude, Grace praised the hospital's generous townsman when he decided to build the home that would improve accommodations for nursing students. Once the Rollins Nurses Home was completed, the student quarters in the hospital were converted into a larger maternity department and children's ward. By 1921, construction of the Rollins Nurses Home was well underway and, for reasons not stated, the hospital sold a portion of the land it had acquired from the Haley estate at a public auction for the sum of $840. The report notes a "substantial fence" was erected as a dividing line between the town of Rollinsford and the city of Dover as if they were enemy combatants, "establishing the boundary of the hospital property and insuring the premises from invasion and possible vandalism."

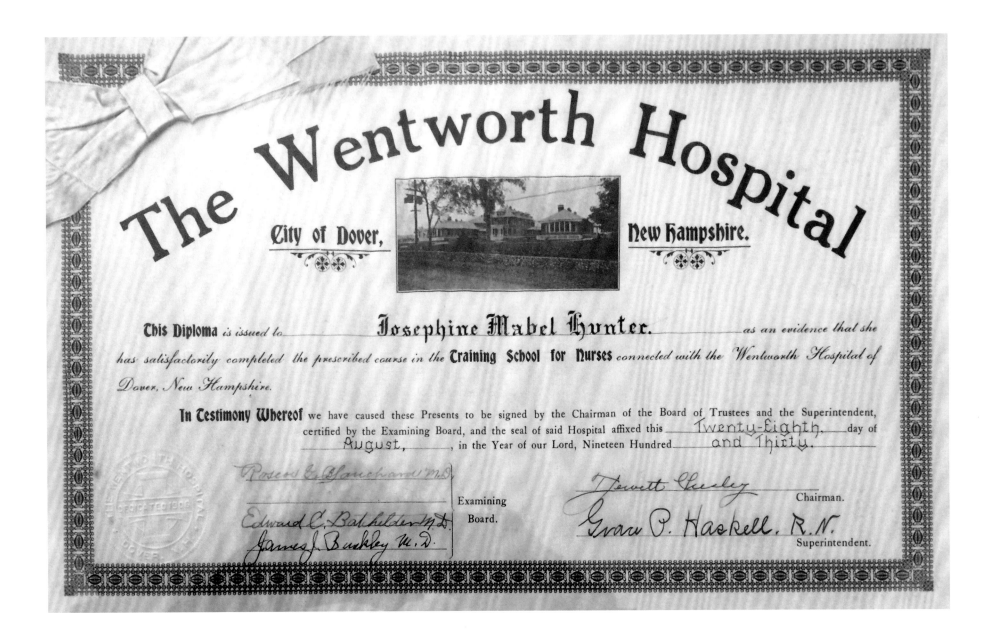

The Wentworth Hospital

City of Dover,   New Hampshire.

This Diploma is issued to _____ Josephine Mabel Hunter _____ as an evidence that she has satisfactorily completed the prescribed course in the Training School for Nurses connected with the Wentworth Hospital of Dover, New Hampshire.

In Testimony Whereof we have caused these Presents to be signed by the Chairman of the Board of Trustees and the Superintendent, certified by the Examining Board, and the seal of said Hospital affixed this _____ Twenty-Eighth _____ day of _____ August, _____ , in the Year of our Lord, Nineteen Hundred _____ and Thirty. _____

Roscoe G. Blanchard M.D.
Edward C. Batchelder M.D.   Examining Board.
James J. Buckley M.D.

Jewett Sweley   Chairman.
Grace P. Haskell. R.N.   Superintendent.

24

Chapter 3: The '20s and '30s

The Roaring '20s saw Yankee Babe Ruth break his home run record and Lindberg cross the Atlantic. Women gained the right to vote in 1920, the same year the 18th amendment passed Prohibition: instigating speakeasies, bootleggers, and the "Jazz Age." The era of flappers and Great Gatsby ended in a crash on Wall Street that sent ruined investors out windows and off balconies to end their agony. A deep and Great Depression spread through the thirties as the "Blues" rudimentary private health insurance took form and Social Security became law.

While the national nonchalance of the twenties seeped through society, Grace Haskell pleaded for better equipment to care for patients and the need to become a Class A hospital. In her 1923 report she asked the city to fund new laboratory equipment, a technician, larger X-ray equipment, and a different system of records for patients. "This I feel strongly should be done but cannot be done without additional expenditures." Her persistence was rewarded in 1925 when funds were allocated to purchase necessary equipment and Wentworth Hospital was designated as a Class A Hospital by the American Hospital Association.

The Great Depression devastated the country and invaded Dover and the hospital. In the 1932 annual report, Mayor Thomas Jewett Chesley referenced a city "shattered on the stock exchange" that resulted in curtailed industrial production. He noted, "man's purchasing power was reduced almost to the point of vanishment" and believed the relief of the unemployed was "the paramount problem facing the city and our nation today." In an unprecedented action, Dover's City Councils implemented a ten percent salary cut for all city employees in April 1933 to include hospital staff. Grace accepted the city's order noting, "the institution would accept the suggested decrease in compensation as a necessary measure in the present financial situation of the country and its various sub-divisions." In her report that same year, Grace thanked the "dedicated doctors" who responded to calls from the hospital without pay. She wrote, "I know no class of men whose time means money, who give so much to the poor whom we have with us always." All salaries were restored in December 1933.

Memories of Grace from Dr. Reid and 106-year old former student

Grace's authority was often challenged by her esteemed male colleagues on the medical staff who dared to confront her. During the hospital's 85th anniversary, Thomas Reid, MD, an elderly, yet feisty retired EENT surgeon, recalled his years at Wentworth Hospital and his tussles with its Superintendent. "I remember Miss Haskell. She was a terror. We lived up here on Washington Street when I first came and then I moved to South Berwick. I was told I wouldn't be allowed to take patients to the Dover hospital so the next day, after I moved, Miss Haskell called me in. She started with 'Dr. Reid...' and I said, 'Now Miss Haskell you better let me talk first. I am gonna live in South Berwick but I am gonna vote in Dover.' I could do that because my family lived here and that was it."

Long before joining the staff, Dr. Reid remembered visiting the hospital by "electric car" and recalled a same-day stay at the other Dover hospital, the Hayes Hospital on Summer Street, to have his tonsils out when he was 10 years old. "It was a private hospital. Dr. Sweeney drove me up in his old Ford, operated on me in the morning, and I came home in a hack. Imagine, I went up in a car and came back in a hack." The Hayes Hospital closed in the thirties.

One of Grace's students from the thirties, Josephine Hunter Stapes, shared vivid memories of Miss Haskell in 2016, at the age of 106, from her lovely home in Danvers, Massachusetts. Although her hearing was not good, her smile was bright and her recollections of the hospital, war years, and current politics were rich in color and substance. A native of New Brunswick, Canada, Josephine proudly showed off her framed nursing diploma signed by Miss Haskell in 1930 and her RN certificate from the NH State Board of Education issued in 1931."Miss Haskell was pretty strict," she said, "but good and I liked her. When a patient rang their bell, we had to be sure they got an immediate answer." Grace did not abide by short hair styles of the era and wanted her nurses to grow their hair long. "She was old fashioned in every way, but we put our hair up and formed curls along the

Josephine Hunter Stapes, RN

sides to make it look short. She really did tell us what to do and we did it."

Grace's health failed as the decades moved on. She submitted a resignation letter in 1927 due to health reasons but was turned down by the Board; they granted her a month-long leave of absence instead. She returned to lead for several more years with a break in 1933 for a "serious operation at the Peter Bent Brigham Hospital in Boston." Her final request to resign was approved, effective May 1, 1937. The Board thanked her for growing the hospital from an "an infant to maturity," and ranking it "high among hospitals and a real benefit to our community."

Ever vigilant, Grace's last report to the city did not mention her retirement but instead she asked the Board to bring their attention to "the urgent need of a new high pressure boiler." She ended her comments with a thank you for the year, but, perhaps, it was for all the years she served as the first administrator. "At this time I wish to thank the personnel of the hospital for the cooperation that has made it possible to do the twenty-four hour daily work of routine, accidents, and emergencies which has made the year a very hard one for all concerned."

Chapter 4: Lily Ford and the Lab

Before Wentworth Hospital opened a laboratory, the only lab in town was in the small office of Roland J. Bennett, MD, at the downtown Masonic Temple building. After meeting with Miss Haskell in early 1925 he agreed to open a lab in the basement of the Rollins Nurses Home, under a back porch in a room "previously used as the luggage room." Dr. Bennett's reflections, in a history he penned years later, bemoaned the lack of lab work at first since "some of the elder doctors were not particularly interested in changing their methods." As the need for blood typing became a valuable resource for surgeons, regular requests began to pour in. In September 1930, a young lady, who came to its lab highly recommended with "excellent qualifications" most notably an "enquiring mind," began a 50-year career at the hospital. That young woman was Lily Ford. Dr. Bennett remarked in his history, "Lily H. Ford continued to advance in her chosen profession as a very dependable and capable young technician and endeared herself to everyone for her dedicated services to the hospital. It was a pleasure to have helped train Lily and to watch her over the years."

Miss Lily Ford, early in her career

Miss Lily Ford in 2002 at the opening of
the Lily Ford Aquatic Therapy Pool.

Interviewed for her 100th birthday, in 2010, Lily Ford, a petite woman with soft white hair and an endearing giggle, recalled her years working in the hospital's lab and subsequent 30 years as a volunteer and member of the Wentworth-Douglass Hospital Auxiliary. Although Dr. Bennett considered her highly qualified, Lily laughed at her inexperience at the time. "I didn't know what the job was," she said, "but I started two weeks later and life was OJT (on the job training) from then on. I was the only one in the lab for years." Miss Ford originally wanted to work at the hospital as a nurse, but found the lab job as a way in and thrived in the environment. She often told this story:

"I was on 24-hour duty every day. Whenever I went somewhere I had to leave my phone number and if there wasn't a phone I had to tell the police where I'd be. I remember one Christmas Eve going to services. I walked down the Avenue to church and at 10:45 p.m. the police came to get me. I was wanted at the hospital. It was a very bad accident. I left the hospital at 3:30 a.m. I never minded being called in. The lab was under the back piazza in the nurses' home. Rain would often come in, so I worked on a platform so my feet wouldn't get wet. We wore white uniforms and we were responsible for them ourselves. They were all starched and pretty sharp back then."

Chapter 5: The '40s, '50s, War, Recovery, Memories

The mid-twentieth century in the United States was dominated by wars that dramatically changed nations. Still grappling with the effects of the Great Depression and clinging to a tentative policy of isolationism, the country was not prepared for the surprise air attack by Japan on December 7, 1941. Over two thousand pilots, sailors, and civilians perished in a few hours that Sunday morning in Pearl Harbor. War was declared the next day.

Because of, and in spite of, the war, the engine of progress moved forward. M&M candies, introduced in 1941, were originally conceived to provide chocolate to the troops that would not "melt" in their hands. The same era saw the intro-

duction of microwave ovens and the marvel of ball point pens when thousands of people "all but trampled one another" at Gimbels department store to spend $12.50 for a new fangled fountain pen. Ernest Hemingway's *For Whom the Bell Tolls* and Dr. Spock's *The Common Book of Baby and Child Care* were the era's bestsellers. President F. D. Roosevelt, like his fifth cousin before him, unsuccessfully asked Congress for an "economic bill of rights," to include adequate medical care coverage, followed by Truman's failed pitch for a national health plan and "single system" for all Americans.

In the 1942 report to the City, Wentworth Hospital Administrator Katherine C. Hall, RN, described a nursing shortage at the hospital due to the war. "The Defense Program and the Red Cross need for army nurses, decreased our staff considerably for we could not hope to compete with the enticing pay and shorter working hours they have to offer." She went on to highlight the high prices and scarcity of many foods. "It is a national concern for us all to eat correctly, to feel well, and do our best work in the war effort."

Nurse Griffin remembers the war years, Rollins Nurses Home

Portsmouth resident and former NH Executive Councilor Ruth Griffin gave up her nurse's license in 2015 when she turned 90. "It was time," she said. She was Miss Lewin in 1943 when she moved into the Rollins Nurses Home at Wentworth Hospital. Her first room was on the third floor where first year students lived, moving later to the second floor as upperclassmen.

They wore denim-blue colored dresses with a white apron and bib. "You couldn't put your bib on until you got your cap in about six months." A black band was added to the white caps when students graduated and became registered nurses. Ruth earned $10 a month for incidentals although the meager stipend could easily disappear she recalled. "If you broke a thermometer you had to pay for it. You had to compensate the hospital for anything you broke." Grace Haskell's rules for nurses were still in effect and followed religiously by her steward, Averil O. Brown, RN. Ruth described her years as a student as rigid but rewarding.

"We worked 12 hours a day and had half a day off. In that 12 hours we were either in class or we were working on the wards, right from the very beginning you were working on the wards. Our little class ended up being about six of us. Evelyn Montiff was hired as a nursing instructor. She came from Peter Bent Brigham and the Haverhill/Amesbury area where Dr. Manning was from. Of course, Dr. Manning was in the service in 1943. Miss Montiff and Dover Mayor Clyde Keefe went to the university (UNH) because there were no doctors to teach the classes because of the war and the university put together a nursing program. We learned all our sciences there. We had real professors right up until the time I graduated. Nursing arts were taught by Miss Montiff down in the basement of the Rollins Nurses Home and we had a room where we could go and smoke. The pharmacy for the hospital was in the basement and Lily Ford was down there too. What a wonderful

Ruth Griffin, RN

woman, she taught us all the blood chemistry and urine chemistry."

Ruth believes the success of Wentworth Hospital came from the dedication of the women who developed and sustained the nursing school. "I'm sure it had been instilled in those women from Miss Haskell, she was so loyal to that hospital. Averil O. Brown and Miss Hoitt - their whole lives were that hospital. Esther Mooney was in charge of the women's ward and Elsie McCloud in charge of the men's ward. Grace Eaton was in charge of the Operating Room. Nobody ever decided they would go somewhere else to work, they were fully dedicated to what they were doing. How unusual it was then and is now. I was damn lucky to have those women around."

It wasn't all work. While the front door to the Rollins Nurses Home was locked each night at 9 p.m., some of the nurses, Ruth included, knew how to slip in unnoticed when necessary. "We had a janitor, he was no bigger than a minute. If you would be late coming home, he would leave the fire escape door open and you could sneak up to get in. I did it a couple of times." The nurses also had a comrade inside the police department. Dick Flynn was a cop in Dover in the forties, Ruth said. "If we were in Dover and it was a quarter to nine and we were in Daeris's Tea Room (3rd St. and Central Ave.) and didn't know how we were going to get up over the hill, he'd put us in the police car, go under the train trestle and take us up so we'd get in the nurses home before 9 o'clock."

The students also did their part for the war effort. Arrangements were made with Camp Langdon in New Castle to invite soldiers to the Rollins Nurses Home. The hospital dietitian made refreshments. "The United States Army brought all these soldiers up and we had a social in that beautiful living room in the Rollins Nurses Home. We couldn't take pictures because we didn't have any film - you couldn't get film during the war. Joyce Richardson played the piano. We entertained the soldiers. We really didn't dance or anything to that extent and we did it more than once." Two of Ruth's classmates met their future husbands at those socials and were married after the war ended.

After graduating, Ruth married and only worked part-time at Portsmouth Hospital (a stone's throw from her house) until her youngest of five children, Tim, started school. She worked in the OR, ER, and as a medical/surgical nurse until the mid-eighties. "The last time I did any floor nursing over at the Portsmouth Hospital, they (patients) would say, 'I would rather have you come in and put me to bed because you know how to do it.' They wanted the old nurses because the old nurses would probably give a back rub, change the draw sheet - they don't even have draw sheets on the beds now, you don't even stay in the bed. It's part of the therapy to heal the person. Wentworth Hospital was certainly a place of healing. It had an excellent reputation. Portsmouth Hospital would recruit nurses from the Dover Hospital. It was an excellent education."

More memories

Family physician Jesse Galt, MD, joined the Wentworth Hospital medical staff in the mid-forties. In 1991 interviews with his colleagues Dr. Lampesis and Dr. Wilson, Dr. Galt recalled what the hospital looked like when he arrived. It was very similar to the original building with two 16-bed wards, one for male and one for female patients with four private rooms in each section. The main building had become the maternity ward. He remarked there was no elevator in that part of the building between the first and second floor. He also remembered an on-call rotation plan devised by the medical staff in the late forties to care for emergency patients. "First call did emergency work at the hospital, second call made emergency house calls in the community. After a few years they reduced call from a month at a time to one week coverage, then set up a roster of one doc each day who came in on-call. Things began to grow and full-time ER docs were hired."

At her 50th anniversary party, Madeline Kennedy laughed about her early days at Wentworth Hospital when she joined the Medical Records department in 1948. "In the beginning, I didn't have a job title. I worked in records and admitting and I relieved the switchboard sometimes. Mary Callahan (RN), was the administrator and Alice Alenty (RN), was the night supervisor. They both had apartments in the nurses home. I think I was called Record Librarian. I worked from 8 to 5 and Saturdays till noon. It was nothing like it is now. We didn't have the facilities or the number of admissions - they didn't have dictation machines then. My sister got me a book on medical dictation and I learned how. Dr. Lampesis still kids me about sitting on Dr. Reid's lap when he dictated. Of course, it's not true."

The '50s
The fifties celebrated hula hoops, the first color TV, and rocked and rolled to a singer named Elvis. New Hampshire's Grace Metalious released her novel, *Peyton Place*, in 1956 selling 60,000 copies in ten days. The Spaulding Turnpike cut through Dover. Medications were more prevalent to treat infections, glaucoma, and arthritis. Salk's Polio Vaccine saved children of the world from death and deformity and the surgeon general issued the first report suggesting cigarette smoking caused cancer.

Peter Lampesis, MD, remembered the fifties as some of his busiest years. "When I first came here, there was only a walk-in entrance in the front of the hospital and eventually a drive-in entrance, where, if you were lucky and got here early enough you could park your car. I can still see that 1950 two-door Chrysler, a big bomb car of Dr. Dan McCooey." The telephone operators and nursing supervisor admitted patients and at night, since they did not have 24-hour operators, the supervisor took over answering the phone along with her other duties. It was a small medical staff in the fifties that relied on specialists from other hospitals. "We didn't have more than 20 people on staff."

Robert Wilson, MD, was the first pediatrician at Wentworth Hospital and one of the founders of the PreNatal Clinic and Strafford Guidance Center. He began a solo practice on Locust Street in 1949 after serving in the Navy, which was interrupted by the 1952 "Doctors Draft" during the Korean War. He returned in 1954 and remained in solo practice until Sol Rockenmacher, MD arrived in 1969. The hospital facilities he recalled, were "disappointing" until they opened the new buildings in the fifties and sixties. Once the last of the old buildings were replaced by modern facilities, Dr. Wilson said things really turned around for the better especially when the hospital separated from the city in the early eighties. "When I first came a larger percent of patients went out of town

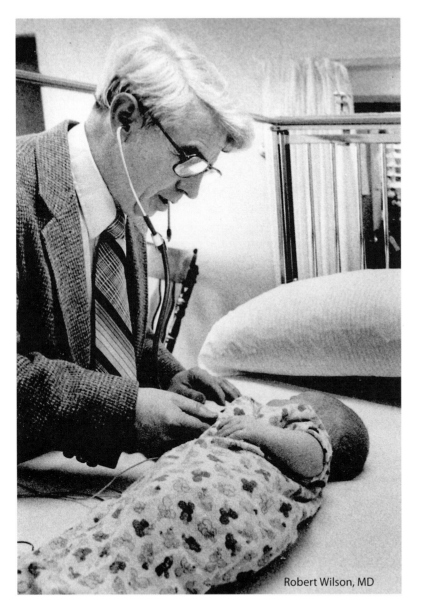
Robert Wilson, MD

for specialized care, since the arrival of specialists, most stayed here."

By 1952, construction of a desperately needed addition began, supported by federal funds, individual donors, and city subsidies, that would add 33 beds and space for support services. It was the same year the nursing school was closed as the demand for the advanced training in nursing became the purview of colleges and universities. At the completion of the project, the hospital changed its name to Wentworth-Dover City Hospital.

The fifties ended with the welcome donation from the estate of Louise B. Douglass that would replace the male and female pavilions and Grace's home, the original administrative building. Mrs. Douglass was the wife of Francis S. Douglass, one of Dover' most respected citizens and a former executive of the American Woolen Company's Dover plant. Under the terms of Mrs. Douglass's will, a trust of approximately one-half million dollars was designated for a new hospital. The balance of funds for the $800,000 construction project came from the Hill-Burton federal loan program.

Chapter 6: The '60s, a Man from Yonkers, Medicare and More

The sixties were famous for a host of firsts: lasers, birth control, men in space, and Star Trek. Unrest among the country's youth resulted in civil rights marches, peace and love sit-ins, women's liberation, and a Beatle invasion. Assassinations of two Kennedys and a King dominated the decade. Man reached the moon. The first heart was transplanted, the first measles vaccine developed, and the first human lung and liver transplants were performed. President Lyndon Johnson signed Medicare and Medicaid into law.

At the Wentworth-Dover City Hospital, an ambitious thirty-year old, born in Yonkers, NY, Vincent J. DeNobile, began a 15-year career as its CEO. Characterized by Board Chairman Vern Webb as a "major force in bringing Wentworth-Douglass to the forefront as a modern, medical complex," and a "financial engineer" for his tight reins of the hospital's finances, he was also well-known as a boisterous Dover Rotarian and active member of the Chamber of Commerce. The local Jaycees selected him in 1963 as "Outstanding Young Man of the

Director Vincent J. DeNobile

Year" lauding him for his work as a hospital leader.

People who remembered DeNobile called him one of the "good old boys." He was a slight man who wore a pale blue leisure suit with aplomb. He had a big heart, strong opinions, and loved to tell jokes. His tight control of the budget irritated some and at least one nurse who knew him said he could be arrogant, yet another thought he was outgoing and friendly. He drove a Rolls Royce and had a fully stocked bar in the back of his office. At a "going away" party in his honor as he left Wentworth-Douglass, William Cusack, MD, described him as "the best administrator" he ever met.

As he focused on reducing expenses, he took charge of three major additions, taking the quiet hospital on the hill to another new, modern era, changing the look and the name once more. The Douglass Memorial wing opened on Sunday, July 30, 1961, bringing the total bed capacity of Wentworth-Douglass Hospital to "90 beds and 24 bassinets." The new building consisted of three stories, plus a basement connected to the Rollins Nurses Home by means of an underground tunnel. At dedication ceremonies, DeNobile praised the 'benevolence of Mr. and Mrs. Francis S. Douglass, the Women's Service Council, the Medical Staff, the many service clubs, and the many other friends of the Hospital, the City of Dover, and its surrounding communities" to make Wentworth-Douglass Hospital "one of the most modern and best equipped hospitals in the State of New Hampshire."

Later in that decade, the hospital received generous donations for two more major additions, from the S. Judson Dunaway Foundation, the same foundation that contributed to Dover's indoor pool at Henry Law Park and to the construction of the South End Fire Station. An Ogunquit philanthropist and former Dover industrialist, Dunaway's first donation funded the Dunaway Pavilion on the south side of the hospital, completed in 1968, bringing the number of inpatient beds to 148. The second addition, the Anna E. Dunaway Wing, parallel to Central Avenue on the north side of the hospital, opened in 1970, adding 30 more beds for a total of 178 - a number that remains the same today. At the Pavilion dedication ceremony, Dunaway told those present that the addition pleased him beyond his "fondest dream." Two years later, at the dedication of the Anna E. Dunaway extended care facility, he addressed 300 attendees with a simple reflection saying, "It is more blessed to give than to receive."

Medicare moves in

Planning for the expansions was serendipitous to a new national demand for hospital beds created in 1965, when Medicare and Medicaid became law. While the fears of over-crowding did not materialize immediately, DeNobile noted a problem that would persist over time. He told a *Foster's* reporter, "The problem that has been encountered relates principally to the paperwork aspects of the program and the ironing out of the bugs that accompany a program of this magnitude."

In a review of the sixties authored by DeNobile, he listed a lexicon of new healthcare terms - intensive care units, extended care facilities and the advent of "regional planning and a comprehensive health plan." The latter would have far reaching impact, forming the underpinnings of the Affordable Care Act of 2010.

As more patients sought care in all forms, the hospital focused on developing comprehensive health care systems, patient education services, and outpatient clinics, including the Diabetes Education Program, the first Pre-natal Clinic in the State, a Well-Child Clinic, TB Clinic, Orthopedic Clinic, Heart Clinic, and Venereal Disease Clinic. During this decade, the first full-time pathologist, Paul C. Young, MD, joined the medical staff and the first electric hospital sign was installed on the front lawn. New construction added "a new pathology department, expanded radiology services, clinic area, conference room, reception area, physical therapy and rehabilitation service area, and new emergency rooms." Emergencies, recorded as 240 visits in 1952, soared to over 6,000 visits in 1968.

Paul Young, MD, Pathology

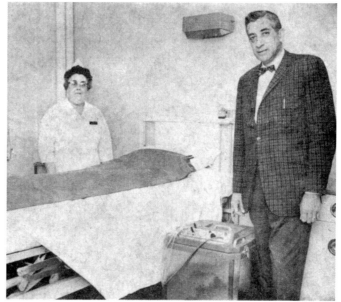

Peter Lampesis, MD, General Practice/Family Medicine

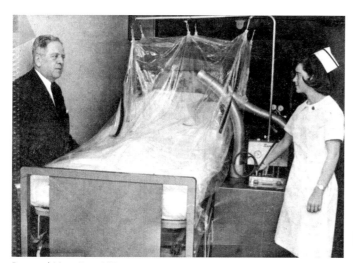

Bernard Manning, MD

Reprinted with permission
from *Foster's Daily Democrat*

Ex-Dover Man Returns To City As Medic

DOVER — Dr. Robert Phillips Hatch has announced the opening of a practice of obstetrics and gynecology in Dover. He is a former resident of Dover, having lived here during the time his father was pastor of the First Parish Church 1930-38.

Dr. Hatch, 36, graduated from Yale University School of Medicine in 1954. He served a one year internship and three years of specialty training at Walter Reed hospital. Since 1958 he has been in Germany at the Second General hospital where he was assistant chief of the obstetric and gynecology service. He has left the army after nine years of active military service, having attained the rank of major.

He is a Diplomate of the American Board of Obstetrics and Gynecology and is a Fellow of the American College of Obstetricians and Gynecologists.

Mrs. Karolin Hatch is a registered nurse who also specializes in obstetrics. She and Dr. Hatch were married in 1952 and have four children: Louise, Douglas, David, and Susan. They will reside at 127 Silver street and Dr. Hatch will have his office in the Rollins Home adjacent to the Wentworth hospital.

Reprinted with permission from *Foster's Daily Democrat*

S. Judson Dunaway (center) breaks ground for Dunaway Pavilion.

Miss Lesley Hoitt, RN, Dir. of Nursing and Vince DeNobile, Director, honor Miss Louise Durgen RN, first graduate of the Wentworth Hospital Nursing School.

Miss Mary Perry (center) with volunteers

Mrs. Seymour Osman (center) with Auxiliary group

Part 2: Rapid Changes – '70s, '80s, '90s

Chapter 7: The '70s, Controversy Brews

Following the sixties hippie era, mini skirts, and moon landings, the seventies took the country on a ride through disco clubs, the neighborhoods of Sesame Street, and a fictional battlefield's mobile army surgical hospital known as MASH. Florida's Walt Disney World opened. Microsoft registered its trademark name for its microcomputer software. The seventies saw the development of a vaccine to prevent rubella, the invention of MRI, CT scanners, and the insulin pump. Before resigning from office, President Richard Nixon renamed prepaid group health care plans as health maintenance organizations (HMOs), with legislation that provided federal endorsement, certification, and assistance.

Interviewed for a Blue Cross publication at the end of the sixties, DeNobile reviewed the past and looked forward to the future. "In the past ten years," he said, "36 new doctors have been added to the staff, which now comprises 84 physicians, including regular staff, consultants, and doctors who are on a courtesy staff basis. The sixties assured a bright future for the health of our community. We view the seventies with accelerated hope and promise." Unfortunately, DeNobile's hopes dimmed as the decade moved on.

The city and the hospital spent the next decade entangled over independence, a battle that raged until the early eighties. As an editorial in *Foster's* proclaimed, one day the hospital would be "flying on its own" quoting Councilman Tuttle, who was looking forward to the day when the city could disband the ties between the city and the hospital, the last city hospital in the state. " I look forward to seeing the cord cut between the city and the hospital within the next year."

Hospital's 75th Anniversary Celebration

Through the mid-seventies, issues percolated from the board room, council chambers, and the news room over the autonomy of the hospital's Board, the City Council's right to know detailed finances, especially salaries, and concern the Board and its administrator were acting too independently. While the city owned the hospital, its management was in the hands of a city-appointed Board of Trustees who hired the administrator and determined the salary for that position. The city manager and mayor were non-voting members of the hospital's Board and frequently criticized for failing to be forthright in their duty to inform the public about the hospital's financial specifics. The more the city demanded the information be released, the more resolute DeNobile and the Board became. Since the hospital no longer required annual financial support from the city, the Board felt budget details were no longer necessary for the city's review. *Foster's*

Daily Democrat was blasted by the Women's Service Council and others for their "distorted reporting" prompting a rare, signed response from the newspaper's publisher Robert Foster on February 7, 1972. He reassured readers the newspaper was focused on neutrality. "Recent meetings of the Wentworth-Douglass Hospital Board of Trustees and the Dover City Council have seen considerable conflict and controversy. We have tried to report these meetings as they happened without slanting or distorting the truth."

Two years later, a news story in the same publication proclaimed, "High Court Says Hospital Winner." The hospital had the right, the court determined, to keep salaries of administrators and employees confidential and affirmed, "the management of the hospital is clearly in the hands of the institution's Board of Trustees."

At the end of 1974, DeNobile announced his plan to resign and move on to become the administrator for Frisbie Memorial Hospital in Rochester, NH, telling a *Foster's* reporter the main reason for leaving the municipal hospital in Dover was the "continued arguments over whether the hospital is subject to city control or would be totally administered by the hospital trustees." Even though the court ruled in the hospital's favor, the city maintained control over the hospital in choosing trustees and securing construction loans for seven more years.

In his final annual report, DeNobile spoke fondly about the hospital that left an "indelible imprint" on his heart and his hopes for the future to be "as bright as the past in delivering the finest health system that we are capable of delivering to the community." He never completely severed his connection to Wentworth-Douglass; in his final administrative years he succeeded in forming an affiliation between Wentworth-Douglass Hospital and Frisbie Memorial Hospital that exists today.

Surgical Center opens, Psychiatric unit opens and closes
A few months after he left, DeNobile's quest to build another addition came to fruition with groundbreaking ceremonies for a six-room surgical center. Orthopedic surgeon Guy Esposito, MD, who joined the medical staff in 1975 after service in the Air Force, recalled the condition of the old surgical suite. "It was just two ORs, a small recovery room, and paint was peeling off the walls. The only reason I stayed is because I knew they were building new ORs. I also knew how great the nursing staff was - that was the real reason I came."

The new wing was dedicated in March 1977 and an estimated 1,200 people toured the $2.4 million addition's operating rooms, central sterilizing room, new pharmacy, a nine-bed recovery room, a holding room, laboratory darkroom for X-rays, and a new central stores warehouse. In September 1976, an employee publication, *Newsoscope*, noted the opening of a six-bed voluntary psychiatric unit to be operated by the hospital and the Strafford Guidance Center. It was located on the "west wing of Douglass 2", next to Pediatrics (near the current 3 West wing), under the direction of John Randall, MD, chief of psychiatry. Admissions to the unlocked unit, the story noted, were "limited to predictable patients." The unit closed two years later, for reasons that may have been more related to cost than trends in care. The new administrator, William Richwagen, said segregating patients into a psychiatric ward had "gone out of style." He said the hospital was "streamlining" its psychiatric services to "mesh with trends in such care, not simply attempting to cut costs."

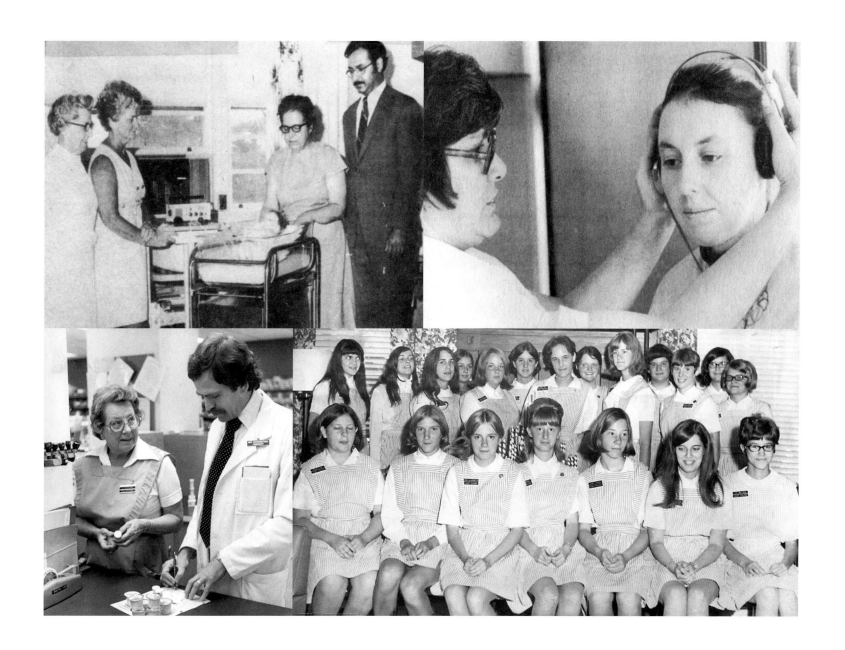

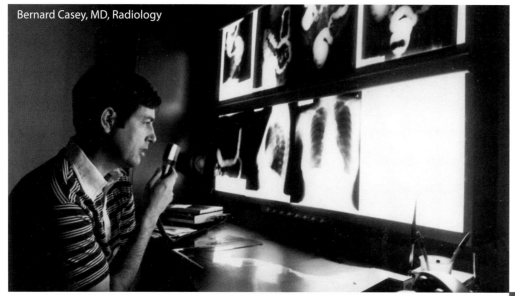
Bernard Casey, MD, Radiology

Richard Bowen, Plant Operations

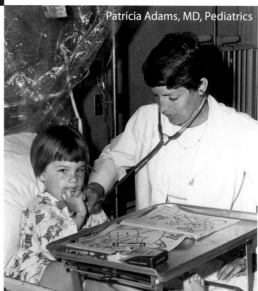
Patricia Adams, MD, Pediatrics

44

Greg Wieder, Materiels and Charles Craven, Administration/Operations

Bea Lempke, Dr. Reid and Alice Alenty, RN

For his 30 years of medical practice in Dover, Dr. Jesse Galt (second from left) was honored last night at the New England Center in Durham by his associates in the medical profession. Also on hand were (from left) Dr. Theodore S. Smith, president of the New Hampshire Medical Society; Hamilton Putnam, executive director of the Society; and Dr. Robert Wilson, of the Wentworth-Douglass Hospital staff.
(Democrat Photo—Richardson)

Dinner Honors Dr. Galt's 30 Years of Service

DURHAM — Dr. Jesse M. Galt was honored for 30 years of distinguished public service to the people of Dover, to the community, and medicine by the Wentworth-Douglass Hospital medical staff at the New England Center last night.

The dinner was attended by more than 100 people including the president of the N.H. Medical Society, Dr. Theodore Smith, the executive director of the N.H. Medical Society, Hamilton Putnam, the trustees, director and medical staff of the hospital and their wives.

Dr. Robert F. Wilson, master of ceremonies presented Dr. Galt with a tape recorder. Dr. Wilson then introduced Dr. John Neff who described Dr. Galt as a "man who personifies what a physician should be in the town he lives and I bring you thanks from Dover."

Dr. Galt has served on the school board for ten years, is a director of St. John's Methodist Church and served as chairman of the building fund committee. He has been president and lieutenant governor of the Kiwanis Club, he has been chairman and director of the United Appeal, director of the Community Concert and has served on many other civic committees.

Mr. Putnam said "Dr. Galt is the only physician who has been elected by his peers twice to serve as president of the N.H. Medical Society."

Dr. Smith presented Dr. Galt a commendation from the society. "Your service to the N.H. Medical Society has been marked by years of effective, meaningful and productive efforts as president in 1966 and again in 1969, as the current Treasurer of the Board of Trustees and for your outstanding service on the House of Delegates, and your dedicated contribution on committees of this Society."

Dr. Galt joined the Wentworth-Douglass Hospital medical staff in July, 1946. A 1936 graduate of Dartmouth College, he attended the Dartmouth School of Medicine and the Emory University School of Medicine, Atlanta, Georgia receiving his medical degree in 1939.

He served a one year internship at St. Joseph's Infirmary, Atlanta, Georgia and a one year internship at Lynn Hospital, Lynn, Mass.

From 1941-1942 he was with the Hitchcock Clinic and was appointed instructor to the Dartmouth School of Medicine. From 1942-1946 he served in the U.S. Army where he received surgical training at the Station Hospital and Tilton General Hospital, Fort Dix, N.J.

In January he was made a diplomat of the American Board of Family Practice awarding him certification as a Family Practioner.

Since joining the Wentworth-Douglass Hospital staff Dr. Galt has served on almost every staff committee and was president of the medical staff from 1956-1960.

Dr. Galt resides with his wife at 600 Central Ave.

Chapter 8: Beckwith to Brown to Richwagen

DeNobile's departure was filled by John Beckwith, 53, former executive director of the Community Center in Scranton, Pennsylvania. He was followed three years later by Norman R. Brown, 65, formerly with Concord Hospital, who took over the Director's chair in April 1978 as an acting executive intent on a short stay.

His ealiest remarks accurately portended his future, when he said, "I'm definitely retired and looking forward to lobster season." Five months later 41-year old William C. Richwagen stepped into the position after leaving posts at Dartmouth Hitchcock Medical Center and the Medical Center of Vermont following his U.S. Army service as an engineering officer.

Administrator John Beckwith

Richwagen loved to talk about skiing, music, cars, his kids, and wife Anne, but not necessarily in that order. He drove an old, bright red, Falcon convertible and reminisced in a 1985 annual report about his background; he was more interested in discussing a 1937 Oldsmobile convertible he owned in high school named Madeline than his extensive qualifications to run the hospital. His goal was "to make WDH a good citizen." He believed the hospital was missing some of the basic medical services he had seen in other communities and felt the structure needed attention. Dr. Esposito described Richwagen as "very analytical and numbers oriented" who "did a lot for the hospital."

A conversation Richwagen had with his director of nursing, summarized the situation facing the new administrator. After a troubling series of bomb threats, a break-in, and growing problems with an ancient boiler plant, she asked him, "When are we going to be a real hospital?" Richwagen's keen interest in making things work found him in the top seat in a backhoe at the 1984 groundbreaking event as the hospital expanded its footprint to add key clinical services that would cast a regional spotlight on a forward-moving hospital.

Administrator William C. Richwagen

Chapter 9: The '80s, Cass Remembers, Adding On

The 1980 Winter Olympics raised the spirits of Olympians and fans nationwide at Lake Placid, NY, when the "Miracle on Ice" US hockey team defeated the Soviet Union. Draped in red white and blue pride, the nation applauded more than the victory on ice, but a victory over a cold war foe. The first successful journey of the Space Shuttle in 1981 was followed, five years later, by the Challenger explosion killing seven people on liftoff including NH school teacher Christa McAuliffe. IBM developed a personal computer and the world wide web made the most mundane and mystifying resources available to anyone with a keyboard and monitor. The eighties saw the development of a Hepatitits B test and vaccine, the antidepressant Prozac, and the first statin drugs. Under President Reagan, Medicare shifted its "fee for service" payment system to one by Diagnosis Related Groups (DRGs) instead of by treatment. Private insurance plans quickly followed suit configuring new capitation payment systems to generally pay doctors and hospitals less than before. Hospitals and physician practices adjusted.

WDH Moves Forward

For the first time, the hospital developed a logo to symbolize "a willingness to change and keep pace with rapidly changing technology." The slate blue graphic was designed as a three winged "Y" reflecting the three parts of "the whole person - body, mind, and spirit." At the heart of the logo was a cross explained in an annual report as "a universal symbol that grew out of Christianity and brotherhood to

represent health care, compassion, and charity for the sick and injured." A stylized cross continues to be at the heart of the hospital's current "beacon" logo. That "Y" shaped logo also modeled the look of the Douglass Building. The main entrance was in the "V" part of the "Y" building. Neurologist and Chief Medical and Integration Officer Paul Cass, DO, recalled his first impression of WDH when he began in 1984. "The first image I had, looking at the hospital, was that sixties 'V' with the center door and the old nursing school from the turn of the century to the right of that building. I remember meetings held in that nursing building. There was a main room with a big fireplace in it. To get to that building, I remember going through a tunnel. Pigeons were living in the upper floors. (Dr.) Karl Sanzenbacker's office was underneath the

Paul Cass, DO

stairs on the left side of the building. He was down where materiel supplies would have been and you walked down that hallway with the pipes and he was underneath the stairway in his office. He built his own evoke potential machine and that's when I came up to take a look before I joined the staff. Karl closed his practice the week before I started. The other person I remember the most was (Dr.) Vito Molori. Vito was often standing or walking with someone. He had a habit of putting his arm around your shoulder because he was a big, bear-like guy. He was Quality Improvement. So when he had his arm around someone, something was going on and he was solving the problem. That's the way I looked at it."

Pam Heal, Switchboard

Karen Lambert, Librarian

Suellen McDonough, RN and H. Jack Myers, MD, General Surgery

Vito Molori, MD, Internal Medicine/Cardiology

Administrators Jeff White and Charles Craven

Ed Eagan, MD, Eye Surgeon   Joannie Blinn, HR   Bill O'Brien, Information Systems

Dan Fogarty, Housekeeping   Martha Cox, RN, Oncology

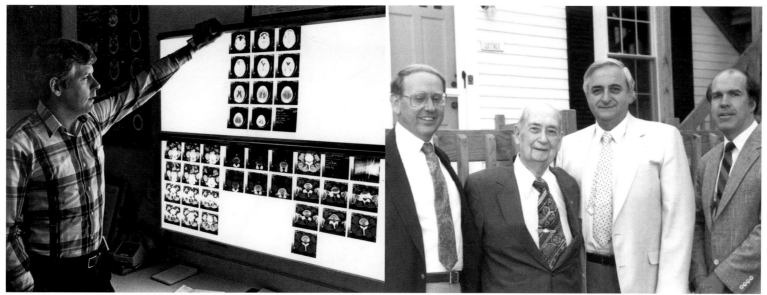

Larry Kane, MD, Radiology

Doctors Joseph Graciano, Thomas Reid, Vito Molori and Paul Berry

(l-r) Linda McKinnon, PR/Volunteers, Paul Butler, MD, General Surgery and Jeff White, Administration.

Auxilian/Trustee Connie Rakoske and Peter Richards, MD

Trustee Andrew Janetos

Henry Sonneborn, MD and H. Jack Myers, MD
discuss patient care with staff

Social Workers Joanne Sirois and Judy Crafts

54

Chapter 10: Separation, Building, Bush Visit

While Dr. Cass navigated the tunnel and Dr. Molori took care of quality, three significant achievements took place at WDH during the eighties. The first, independence, involved the ongoing and finally successful effort to separate from the city; the second, construction, created the largest additions and most extensive expansion of services to date, including emergency and oncology, and the third, relationship building, began an era focused on partnership, cost-containment, and service.

NH Gov. Hugh Gallen signs HB831 separating the hospital from the city in 1981

HB831, signed into law by Gov. Hugh Gallen on July 11, 1981, removed "the legal and administrative confusion of Wentworth-Douglass Hospital's quasi municipal status" and established "the hospital as a non-profit community hospital similar to that of 24 other New Hampshire hospitals." The law created a board of 60 corporators made up of 45 citizens of Dover and 15 from surrounding communities." A later bill sponsored by WDH Trustee and State Representative Ann Torr, allowed WDH to amend its charter and identified the hospital as a "non-profit entity," expanding the hospital's geographic area by eliminating the restrictions of appointments to only Dover residents. The 1989 law contained an absolute prohibition on transfer of the hospital to a for profit entity. It stated, "No action may be taken by the board of trustees, to dissolve, liquidate, consolidate, merge or transfer all of the assets of the corporation to other than an organization or organizations which are then organizations exempt from federal income taxation under the Internal Revenue Code, including but not limited to the City of Dover."

The process took years to accomplish and pitted city politicians against each other and hospital trustees, stirring up a community looking for a cause. The news began with a commentary in a *Foster's* news story on July 9, 1980, noting Wentworth-Douglass Hospital trustees were "again seeking to change the constitution of their hospital" referencing that "sources indicate increased independence from the city is the objective." The Strafford County Legislative Delegation and Dover City Council received a letter, signed by Pauline Soukaris, chairman of the Wentworth-Douglass Board of Trustees, inviting them to a conference "to review an initial proposal for changes in the hospital's constitution." Ms. Soukaris referred to "the stormy history of hospital, delegation and council relations" but the board did not anticipate any disputes this time in seeking constitutional changes. "In looking to the future of the hospital and the area it serves - over half of its patients now come from outside Dover," Ms. Soukaris said, "we would like to resolve some areas of confusion over its status."

In response to a reporter, state Rep. Leo Lessard, D- Dover, chairman of the Strafford County Legislative Delegation, said he believed it was an "inappropriate" time for proposed changes in the hospital constitution. Rep. George Maglaras, D-Dover, chairman of the Dover Legislative Delegation, said, "Every two years there's some hassle about who owns the hospital," adding that although he believed increased "disassociation" from the hospital was probably a good move, there were a lot of people who still felt the city should own the hospital. A few months later, in an editorial entitled, "Free Wentworth-Douglass", an editor commented, "The time is ripe - probably overdue - for Wentworth-Douglass Hospital to cut its dried up umbilical cord to the city of Dover." Discussion continued with back and forth comments from the Dover delegation vs. Dover City Council. Another editorial suggested, "The Dover delegation should not be involved in the hospital issue at all." It stated the hospital issue was between the hospital Board of Trustees and the Dover City Council and "the delegation enters the picture only because an act of the New Hampshire House is required to sever the remaining ties between the hospital and the city."

The ultimate legislation, sponsored by Phyllis DeNafio, Theresa DeNafio, and Frank Torr, succeeded in the end. Frank Torr recalled the conflict. "Some felt the city should never give away a valuable asset." He felt the obligation for the hospital's Board to seek approval from the city for trustee appointment and bond issues were increasingly difficult due to an ever changing council and the hospital's interest in expanding programs beyond Dover to the wider seacoast area. "I can remember the debate on the floor, it was a bitter debate," Torr said. "I felt it (separation) was a good thing to do. I know the hospital would not have been able to do the things it has done over these many years if they had not pushed for independence."

Trauma designation

As the politics for independence ended, the hospital took another step forward with its designation as a regional trauma center by the Emergency Medical Service, a division of the New Hampshire public health service. In 1982, hospital spokesperson Mary Perry noted Wentworth-Douglass joined Exeter Hospital on the trauma center list earlier that spring. Ms. Perry said, "Wentworth-Douglass and Exeter Hospitals were chosen as trauma centers after a survey team of administrators, doctors, and nurses from Pease Air Force Base visited the hospitals in the region. Because the region is geographically split into two areas, Dover and Rochester to the north, Portsmouth and Exeter to the south, two units were chosen."

Construction - State Approval

That same year the hospital added its first CT scanner and began plans to construct a major addition. In a unanimous decision, the New Hampshire State Bureau of Institutional Health Services Review Board gave Wentworth-Douglass Hospital "approval to proceed with plans for the installation of a regional radiation therapy center." The Bureau gave final approval for a $23 million expansion project noting, "the granting of the certificate means that hospital officials can go ahead with plans to expand a number of services at W-D, including a larger trauma center, consolidation of two separate intensive care units, to improve and expand the

maternity and neonatal care unit, to modernize the hospital's heating plant, and include space for a regional radiation therapy center, the only new service included in the proposal."

"Dig into the future" ground-breaking ceremonies were held in November 1984. Sixty first-graders donned plastic hard hats, picked up small shovels and dug into mounds of dirt to begin the ceremonies. The students were from among 400 local youngsters who participated in a coloring contest about hospital care. The addition opened two years later with a new main entrance facing east toward Rollinsford.

(l-r) Administrator William Richwagen, Barbara Bush, Trustee Ann Torr, VP George H. W. Bush and Board Chairman Francis Robinson

VP Bush and Barbara visit

Trustee Ann Torr recalled that bright fall day when the Dover High School Green Wave band played "Hail Columbia" as Vice President George H. W. Bush and his wife Barbara entered the striped tent where 3,000 people gathered for dedication ceremonies. "I remember the background behind the VP had to be blue. There were secret service and advance people surrounding the hospital. I was seated right next to George Bush and presented a book to Barbara. It was a great day." VP Bush singled out Wentworth-Douglass for its contribution of "hope for today's society." He remarked how hospitals once were prepared only to make the final days of an ill person easier. But, as research added to medical knowledge in the modern society, the purpose of a hospital evolved from "reacting to illness to anticipating illness, offering cures and prolonging good health following treatment."

Hospital Board Chairman Francis Robinson's remarks sent a message of gratitude to the hospital staff. "The heart of a hospital is not a building. The heart of a hospital is the hearts and hands of those who work in it and for it…the hearts of nurses who care, the skilled hands of doctors who heal, and the help of many, many others who maintain the building and its equipment and who aid those hearts and hands as they carry on their comforting work."

Chapter 11: Cardiology, Coming Together

Cardiac care became another excellence endeavor in the mid-eighties with the opening of the first cardiac catheterization lab and expanded cardiac rehabilitation. A third floor addition in '88 added more space to care for patients with heart problems in the new Douglass North telemetry unit. During the center's open house, cardiologist William Danford, MD, gave demonstrations on the progression of pacemakers while head nurse Liz Black, RN, demonstrated the new telemetry system. The annual report that year featured a story about a heart attack victim, written by emergency nurse Gail Wasiewski, RN.

"I'll never forget this patient and his wife. She never interfered with treatment and never gave up hope. Finally, she asked the physician,'Why is he so cold?' Suddenly, just as she spoke, the monitor blipped and went from a flat line to an active rhythm. He was still unconscious and unresponsive but he was alive…No one is sure just what happened - the ambulance crew's consistent CPR, our own staff's skill and persistence, a trauma room full of the best equipment and most modern technology, the patient's fighting will to live, a steady stream of answered prayers, or the soft, love-filled voice and touch of his wife. Or was it all of these?"

While Richwagen focused on making the hospital a strong contender in a competitive marketplace, some members of the medical staff focused on a more playful competition. Key participants were interviewed about a 1983 Annual Fun Run

Cardiology Committee

Dr. Graciano at 1983 Fun Run

held during National Hospital Week. Paul Butler, MD, placed first, followed a second later by Richard Petrie, MD, who said he felt the competition was "an excellent way to help the hospital promote good health habits." About 25 children also "ran, walked and skipped" that year and two of the youngest, daughters of Joseph Graciano, MD, were pushed to the finish line "in a stroller in 36 minutes by their fit and fast dad."

Relationships

In an effort to work within the changing payment systems and to reach beyond the "small community hospital" focus of the past, WDH began to build relationships with other providers, hospitals, and health systems. One of the first of many relationships established over the years began with affiliation discussions between the Boards of Frisbie Memorial Hospital (FMH) and Wentworth-Douglass.

In 1984, FMH President Vince DeNobile said, "experts in the health care field say any hospital under 300 beds is not going to make it by 1990." William Richwagen added, the affiliation was the "coordination and promotion of a regional health care system, which should result in lower health care costs for both communities." The hospitals formally authorized the affiliation between the two health care facilities in September 1985 and christened the new corporation Health Circle, Inc. Earlier in the year the two hospitals took a first step in a tightened relationship with the creation of Strafford Health Alliance, a joint venture to buy a mobile van for low dose mammography. A naming contest at both hospitals resulted in the name Women's Life Imaging Center. The service began operation, alternating hospital locations then moving to a fixed location on Rt. 108 in 1986. Later that year Strafford Health Alliance created rehab services at Marsh Brook in Somersworth. Women's Life and Marsh Brook remain joint ventures today.

By the end of the decade, talks to move even closer through a merger began to falter as local control issues surfaced and unexpected changes in leadership disrupted discussions. Vince DeNobile suffered a debilitating heart attack and never resumed his role as CEO of Frisbie Memorial Hospital. William Richwagen left his position at WDH in June 1989 and went on to other leadership positions in health care, later retiring to ski full-time in Vermont.

Chapter 12: The '90s, Gabarro Arrives, Physicians Group, Partners Form

The tragedy of war and internal unrest returned to the country in the early nineties as Iraq invaded its neighbor, Kuwait, and the U.S. initiated Operation Desert Storm, ending in 1991. By the end of the decade a new term, Google, was registered as the domain name of the new search engine google.com. The word was chosen by two Stanford grads as a play on the word "googol," a mathematical term for the number represented by the numeral 1 followed by 100 zeros reflecting they wrote, "a mission to organize a seemingly infinite amount of information on the web." They succeeded. The nineties saw the arrival, in 1996, of the Health Insurance Portability and Accountability Act known as HIPAA, a law developed to protect patient privacy. Health care costs rose at double the rate of inflation while the expansion of managed care helped to moderate increases in health care costs. Another attempt at federal health care reform legislation failed again to pass in the U.S. Congress during the Clinton Administration.

A 41-year old Ralph Gabarro left his post as vice president of operations at Mid-Maine Medical Center, in Waterville to fill the vacancy left by Richwagen. A gregarious leader, he was seldom in his fourth floor office and could be found roaming around on any floor, at any time, even in the middle of the night talking to third shift staff, listening to their stories, and telling a few of his own. He wrote a weekly column in the employee newsletter, called "The Open Door" to be sure employees knew the hospital's business before the local media.

He had been hopeful the work of his predecessor and others on the boards of the Dover and Rochester hospitals would result in a cost-savings combination of some sort but a special meeting of all parties revealed the boards were at an impasse. In one of the first issues, on June 11, 1990, he informed employees of the results of talks between WDH and FMH. "It was apparent," he wrote, "that Trustees, Medical Staffs, and Administrations do not favor a full merger of both hospitals at this time. " At a later date, Trustee Ann Torr told reporters, "It was just very evident that the timing was not right for a merger."

Trustees Ronald Henderson and Roger Evans, MD meet with Hospital President Ralph Gabarro

While the hospitals, insurers, and legislators dealt with the cost of health care, WDH kept pace with new technology and the demands of consumers, focusing on program expansion, adding more medical practices and developing new relationships. In November 1993, WDH opened the Seacoast Cancer Center, a unique program that combined medical and radiation oncology services in one location. At the ribbon cutting ceremony Gabarro said, "This is a proud moment. We're expanding on our already excellent programs." He also mentioned his son Peter, who had an inoperable brain tumor and told the attendees that cancer affected his family, noting cancer was an "intimidating disease," a disease that "affects us all at one point in our lives or another." Mayor Patricia Torr, who assisted in the ribbon cutting, said the center "continues to make this community very proud."

New Directions

In 1994 Wentworth-Douglass Hospital merged with Squamscott Visiting Nurse and Hospice Care "to improve continuity of care." Home Care Department Director Nancy Boyle, RN, said hospitals needed to "participate in health care beyond the hospital walls." In order to manage costs of home care more effectively, the hospital later formed a joint venture with Integricare (that became Amedysis) to manage the agency. The named of the agency changed to Wentworth Homecare & Hospice and continues to care for patients throughout the Seacoast.

The hospital's walls stretched even farther as it acquired the The Works Athletic Club in 1995. A concerted effort by local employers and insurers to reward their employees for regular participation in exercise programs, made the purchase of the Somersworth business a natural progression in the managed care environment from caring for the sick to helping people prevent illness. An Integrative Therapy Committee, formed a year later, was conceived, in part, to augment programming available at The Works. According to Barry Gendron, DO, chairman of the committee, he worked closely with Vice President of Nursing Karen Stensrud, RN, and other hospital staff to integrate programs at the Works that would be consistent with the hospital's values. The Works was purchased shortly after Dr. Gendron met with Ralph Gabarro to discuss the potential of the facility. "I believed it was a great investment for the hospital and it has turned out that way," Dr. Gendron said.

The Works expanded through the years, added a family focus and programs targeted at living with diabetes, cancer, and preventing obesity, becoming The Works Family Health & Fitness Center.

Practice Acquisition

During the eighties the hospital opened its first hospital-owned medical practice, Care Connection, in a plaza in Durham, NH. The practice eventually grew and moved to another location in Durham, the Durham Health Center on Madbury Road. By 1994, the hospital understood the need to employ physicians and acquire practices to insure access to primary care. The Wentworth-Douglass Physician Corporation was formed that year, reorganized as a department of the hospital in 2005 called Wentworth Health Partners. Soon after Peter Walcek took on the role of Vice President of Finance, he recalled that one of the challenges facing the hos-

Thomas Decker, MD

pital was practice acquisition. "One of our biggest struggles was should we jump into employing physicians - if you don't have patients you don't have a business." Eventually, administration made the jump, understanding the additional expense would be offset with patients staying in the community as more doctors were available to care for them. By December 2015, Wentworth Health Partners included 14 primary and 20 specialty practices in 8 communities throughout the seacoast area with over 350 dedicated employees including 120 providers.

Dr. Decker's story about the good and not-so-good old days
Internal medicine specialist Thomas Decker, MD, talked about his shift from being an independent physician to becoming an employee of Wentworth Health Partners in a 2012 Windows magazine. "In the early days everybody did everything, even specialists did some primary care. I even moonlighted in the ER. We worked 75 hours over 7 days, took call, worked weekends and nights. I didn't mind too much in the beginning, at least it was less than the 100 hours a week we worked in residency. It was very intoxicating back then. I would go into the hospital and make an impact, change things. We began to get new equipment and could take care of patients in the unit and no longer needed to ship patients out. Then the cardiology group came in and we had

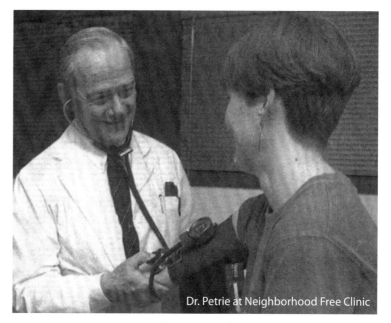
Dr. Petrie at Neighborhood Free Clinic

new surgeons - it was really a time of exceptional growth. It was nerve racking too. We were in the office, then back to the hospital doing rounds and we had night call. It was very time consuming – we had lots of divorces in the medical staff. Now (with hospitalists specializing in inpatient care) we have a better division of labor. We don't have to be in two places at once. I'm pretty happy as an employed physician. I can spend more time with my patients. It's more predictable. Life is better."

Affiliations and more
During the nineties, the Wentworth-Douglass Hospital Board of Trustees signed memorandums of understanding with potential partners seeking to contain the escalating

costs of health care. The first compact, announced in 1994, known as the United Community Health System, involved six hospitals: Concord, Southern NH Medical Center, Cheshire, Mary Hitchcock (Dartmouth), Cooley Dickinson of Northampton, Mass and WDH. It dissolved due to a lack of a common organizational structure and the unwillingness by all parties to relinquish local control. A second affiliation effort in 1997 with Optima Healthcare also ended within one year.

Wentworth-Douglass Hospital continued to seek partners over the years, carefully analyzing the risks and the rewards, resulting in successful relationships as a new century took form. Some examples included the the Neighborhood Free Clinic, inspired by Richard Petrie, MD, that offered free primary health care one night a week through the combined efforts of the hospital and The Clinic, a community health and social service center. The program closed when primary health services for low income, uninsured community members opened at The Clinic, now known as Goodwin Community Health. Later in the decade a new "Books for Babies" collaboration with Wentworth-Douglass Hospital, Healthy Universal Beginnings also known as the HUB, and the Dover school district came together to give every newborn a book to inspire early learning. Soon after a birth, while still in the hospital, a new mother received a children's book and a letter from School Superintendent Gerald Daley, officially welcoming the baby into the "Community of Learners." The program, funded by the WDH Auxiliary, has evolved over the years and continues through the support of the WDH Auxiliary Endowment Fund.

Loss and Change

Ralph Gabarro's 12-year old son, Pete, lost his battle with cancer in 1994. Sadness seeped out of Pete's room on Pedi that day, affecting so many who knew the CEO and his family. In Pete's memory, members of the medical staff and hospital staff organized the first Pete Gabarro Memorial Golf Tournament, held on June 13, 1995 at Cochecho Country Club. Proceeds over the next 16 tournaments supported Children's Care Projects at Wentworth-Douglass Hospital including educational conferences and Pete's Place counseling services for children dealing with the death or chronic illness of a loved one. Funds raised through the tournament served to comfort families, as well as classrooms of students sharing the tragic loss of a friend or family member. Tournament proceeds also supported an Asperger's Syndrome program, developed at Somersworth High School. to provide support and tools for better communication between all students.

In the fall of 1996, Ralph Gabarro left his position as President of WDH. He returned to Maine where he served as a hospital CEO, retiring in 2014.

Awards banquet

Douglass South Care Team

(l-r) Dee Rusczyk, Betty Smith, Ralph Gabarro and Diana Rutherford

65

Chapter 13: Walker Era Begins, Rollins, Memories

A gentleman from Portland, Oregon, Walter Behn, succeeded Gabarro as Interim CEO. He was known for his easy going manner, love of good food, and Kudos. He carried a supply of the candy bars and threw them at anyone caught in a good deed. Behn served as Interim CEO for seven months prior to the board's selection of New Jersey executive Gregory Walker as the next President & CEO of WDH. "We wanted someone who could demonstrate a high level of integrity. Greg has come to us highly recommended," Robert DeColfmacker, Board Chairman said. "His experience matches our needs." Prior to his arrival, Walker was vice president of operations and chief operating officer at The Memorial Hospital of Salem County Inc., in Salem, New Jersey. A native of Schenectady, New York, Walker received his bachelor of science degree in biology from Niagara University and a master's degree in health administration from Xavier University.

WDH President & CEO
Gregory Walker

Frequently described as a visionary, this tall, thoughtful executive has gained the respect of employees and the medical staff even when he takes his time to consider a new idea or make an important decision. Dr. Esposito described Walker as a leader who understands a lot about medicine, "more than any CEO I've worked with." He also believes the health system's executive has "a real warm center..a real sense of right and wrong." When he served as Chief of Surgery, reporting to Walker, Dr. Esposito learned to be ready to present his case. "If you want to convince Greg about something you've got to be prepared, you've got to have your numbers. He's on the cutting edge of most of the trends...he's very open to new ideas."

Walker's been known to go out of his way to help a lost visitor and wish good morning to volunteers on his morning trip for a cup of tea. His fourth floor office has the look of someone interested in order and early on, it housed architectural sketches of what he thought the hospital could be. At his five-year service award ceremony, two trustees enjoyed roasting him for his impeccable taste and ever-present cuff links. He laughed with everyone and said how proud he was to just be one of the many employees honored that evening.

Rollins Building Demise

As the nineties came to a close at Wentworth-Douglass Hospital, teams of employees successfully prepared for a new century and the year 2000 (Y2K). It was also the year the last vestige of historical buildings, the Rollins Nurses Home, came down to make way for a series of expansions continuing Wentworth-Douglass Hospital's journey to excellence. After the nursing school closed in 1952, the building was subsequently used for medical practices, a library, the offices of staff education, accounting, community relations and, at the very end, as a fitness center for employees. The last nurse to live in the Rollins building was Alice Alenty, until it was determined by the city to be a fire hazard. Costs to renovate the 1922 structure for contemporary uses were far more than costs of new construction. Reaction to its demise were mixed, most were understanding, others wistfully remembering another era, long ago. The portrait of Gladys Rollins was moved to the hospital's fourth floor. Bricks were salvaged from the building and inserted in the base of the new brick sign constructed on the corner of Old Rollins Road and Central Avenue. Other bricks were given away to employees as mementos. Former Assistant Director of Nursing Doris Noyes, RN, remembered the day the Rollins building came down. "I was really sad when they tore it down. I still have a brick with a little brass plate that says Rollins Building. I use it as a door stop. I understood the necessity but it made me really sad because I loved that building." Ruth Griffin said she has a couple of bricks as well.

Docs remember
Three long-term physicians retired in the nineties leaving words of wisdom and remembrances. Family medicine physician Jesse Galt, MD, retired after 50 years of service noting how glad he was when emergency docs came along. "Some GPs grumbled about the new specialists on the block, for the most part they were welcome, especially emergency doctors." Peter Lampesis, MD, left after 43 years practicing in Dover, noting changes over time. "I don't see as many doctors mak-

ing house calls. I didn't mind … if people could not get out. I probably did fall asleep a few times at the office though." He also spoke about improvements in caring for patients with diabetes, "We used to see a number of people lose their vision or have legs amputated as a result of complications from the disease. We're now able to save many lives and limbs."

The hospital's first full time surgeon, Roger Temple, MD, retired after 29 years of service at Wentworth-Douglass Hospital. He said he enjoyed the association with the people in the hospital the most and would not miss "the pressures of a managed care environment and being on call." "Anesthesia," he said, "made our hospital a very safe place. We haven't had the ups and downs of other hospitals. It's been very steady improvement here."

Roger Temple, MD

Part 3: The Early 21st Century (2000-2016)

Peace continued to elude the early 21st century. The 911 tragedy shattered a nation and its ramifications continue an insidious spread. Bombings, beheadings, and malevolence around the world took breaths away and left insecurity in its wake. The natural dramas of hurricanes, floods, and earthquakes took lives and homes and dreams away. The unnatural dramas of school shootings and community violence broke hearts and made a nation wonder why. This was the same era when technology soared. Android made touch screens come to life and Apples grew in every format from pods to pads, to phones and watches. Kindles and e-readers turned books into digital formats and corner bookstores close to obsolescence. Google became a verb. Texting became digital conversation. Scientists successfully mapped the human genome identifying human genetic variations that may be the key to treating disease. And, it was a time when government and health care collided on the political stage in a drama that became a law, the Patient Protection and Affordable Care Act of March 2010.

Chapter 14: Becoming the Seacoast's Leading Medical Center

The hospital's tag line, *The Seacoast's Leading Medical Center*, was the result of broad input from the Board of Trustees, administration, medical staff, employees, patients, and community. Developed in the first year of the 21st century, it was more than a marketing slogan or an aspirational target; the statement described a hospital already leading the Seacoast in the number of patient care services offered. It connected the past, filled with Grace Haskell's desire to be an "A" hospital, to the visions of administrators and boards to do the best for the community. Greg Walker recalled his earliest impression of the hospital.

"I remember when I walked in the front door how people smiled at me and asked me where I was going and took me to the conference room for my interview. It told me that this hospital had the core of something special and it had a special workforce. It looked old and tired, the nurses' residence was on the corner and it wasn't being utilized but there was a sense of pride in the hospital, pride in the community. The hospital needed to have a vision of not what it had been but what it could be in the future. We needed to bring new physicians, new services to this community so we wouldn't have to refer patients out. People could stay in the local community and stay at this hospital."

Dr. Paul Cass described these early 21st century years as a period when the medical staff got together, under Walker's leadership, and decided to look at tertiary partners. "That was very innovative thinking," he said, attributing the momentum for physician leadership to both the former and current CEO. "Ralph Gabarro was the first one who said we should have a physician in the executive suite because without that we could not have the right input - again, innovation. We've been fortunate that way."

Vice President of Patient Care Services and CNO Sheila Woolley, RN, left the bustle of a Dallas children's hospital to move to New Hampshire closer to family and remembered, similar to Walker's first memories, that the hospital felt small and "antiquated" when she first arrived. She soon fell in love with the people she met, their enthusiasm for change, and the CEO's commitment to excellence. "I moved here because of the people and Greg," she said. "He had a vision to improve the quality, expand services; he understood the necessary collaboration with physicians and nurses. He tore down the past and really brought us into a new century."

Construction: Chaos to completion

The sight of cranes, hard hats, detours, and drilling marked the early 21st century at WDH. Major additions touched the north, south, east, and west perimeters. Walker believed the construction that added square feet and new dimensions to the hospital was the result of years of building within the medical staff. As the hospital recruited more specialists, surgeons, general internists, and medical subspecialists volume went up and space ran out. "We added the ambulatory building, wound, sleep medicine, and outpatient surgery - all have grown tremendously," he said. "We've been able to add a number of medical oncologists and medical oncologic subspecialists which has really pushed the growth of the Seacoast Cancer Center and we've got an incredible radiation oncology group. We were the first hospital that did IMRT (Intensity Modulated Radiation Therapy) in the state." Smaller hospitals developed referral networks with us for oncology, pediatric subspecialty care, and other services. "All those things have created a draw for patients to come to Wentworth-Douglass."

The first phase of a $20 million expansion was completed in 2002. NH Governor Jeanne Shaheen joined Greg Walker on a warm August day to cut the ribbon for the new Ambulatory Building addition featuring a fixed MRI, Same Day Surgery, Endoscopy, and the Lily Ford Aquatic Therapy Pool in the new, sun-filled Rehabilitation Services Center.

Endoscopy - Flavin remembers

The Ambulatory Building's Center for Advanced Endoscopy was the third location for the service. Gastroenterologist David Flavin, MD, remembered the original service begun by Geoff Clark, MD, in one room at the back of the old Emergency Department (ED) next to the fledgling oncology service. "When I started in 1981 with Geoff Clark and Helen Kincaid (RN), we were next to Henry Sonneborn's group. The hospital didn't own its own endoscopes so we brought our own. We did primary diagnostics - about 2,000 a year. Then we moved to the area currently used by Emergency as a holding room." The space, designed by the physicians, was too small, almost from the beginning. Dr. Flavin laughed because he admitted the physicians "didn't have the vision to predict how busy we would be."

Ambulatory Building 2002 ribbon cutting. (l-r) Board of Trustees Chairman Roger Evans, MD, President & CEO Gregory Walker, Trustee Gerald Daley, Trustee Janet Perry, NH Gov. Jeanne Shaheen, NH Sen. Katie Wheeler, NH Rep. Iris Estabrook, NH Exec. Councilor Ruth Griffin and Trustee Malcolm McNeill.

The current center features a spacious holding room and four procedure rooms, one dedicated to endoscopic retrograde cholangiopancreatography, or ERCP, used to study the bile ducts, pancreatic duct, and gallbladder. Wentworth-Douglass Hospital's ERCP room also has its own fluoroscopy unit. Dr. Flavin emphasized the value of this program begun by Rob Ruben, MD, as "high level" and "very unusual in a community hospital." He added, "WDH has the only High Resolution Esophageal Motility testing and Esophageal Impedance testing in the Seacoast, championed by Rob Ruben to assess esophageal function."

The center's gastroenterologists expanded their repertoire of procedures from basic diagnostics to also include Endoscopic Ultrasound, implemented by Jamie Baquero, MD, and advanced therapeutic applications including the removal of gall stones and Barrett's esophagus ablation to prevent the progression of esophageal cancer. While the population in the area has increased during this time, the value of screening colonoscopies has gained national attention and increased volume. "We're finding cancer earlier and the death rate from colon cancer has definitely declined. We're really growing - over 7,500 cases per year now."

New Spaces
The second phase of construction, on the opposite side of the hospital, created another new main entrance, facing Rollinsford and an expanded parking garage. The most striking feature upon entering the building was the 33-foot polished granite waterfall carved in the shape of the Granite State. It was designed for a dual purpose, to muffle private

conversations and create a place for relaxation and healing. The building project also created a separate entrance for the Seacoast Cancer Center and new treatment space for a new linear accelerator. A year later, a new specialized cancer treatment program was available called high dose rate (HDR) brachytherapy. President Walker said the hospital had seen a demand for some services growing 40 to 50 percent. "It's been tremendous growth over the past three or four years."

The Emergency Department expanded on the north side of the hospital and the Douglass building "V" was filled in with an appealing curved structure to provide for a new inpatient unit, 3 West, on the third level and the Rollins Educational Center on the fourth floor, named in recognition of the Rollins family's contributions to the hospital. Where possible, the design of new spaces included massive windows often filling entire walls in patient care areas with natural light. The need for light and air, as CNO Sheila Woolley explained, harkened back to Florence Nightingale, who knew its intrinsic value when she wrote in the late 1800s, "The craving for the return of the day, which the sick so constantly evince, is generally nothing but the desire for light."

ChaD at WDH

Curved walls, floating clouds, animal foot-printed ceilings, and dragonfly lights chased conventional hospital design away with the addition of the children's center on the third level of the Ambulatory Building. In a collaborative agreement with Children's Hospital at Dartmouth (CHaD), the new CHaD at WDH opened in 2007 to provide pediatric specialty medicine for local families and save long distance travel to other medical centers. Naomi Gauthier, MD, pediatric cardiologist and one of the pioneers of ChaD at WDH, was recognized for her contributions by the New Hampshire Hospital Association in 2014 with the Outstanding Medical Staff of the Year Award.

Center for Pain Management

The Center for Pain Management originated as a part-time service in 1995 then moved to a full-time program next to CHaD on the third level of the Ambulatory Building, using innovative injection and pain management techniques to quell chronic or unrelenting pain. Anesthesiologist and pain specialist James McKenna, MD, emphasized the center's high standards to help patients control pain. "Primary care physicians and surgeons refer their patients who have problems with pain control. We use nerve blocks and variety of therapies - physical therapy too. We never initiate narcotics to treat pain but we do work with patients already on narcotics. We try, if possible, to get patients off these drugs or cut them down. Years ago people were under treated and then the pendulum went the other way and people were over treated. We're the only in-hospital pain center in the area. Unlike free standing pain centers, we have peer review and quality standards we have to meet. We are extremely unique."

The Garrison Wing Project

The four-story Garrison Wing opened in January 2013, named in honor of Dover "the Garrison City" and dedicated to education and healing. The hospital's largest addition curved close to the edges of Central Avenue and prompted Board of Directors Chairman Roger Hamel to describe the new wing as bringing "the hospital to the street." He said, "Before, the hospital was there but a lot was in the back, behind a facade, now it stands out there and it is very visible and very impressive." Hamel's familiarity with Wentworth-Douglass goes back to his years as an auditor, followed by a period as a cancer patient in the late nineties. "I was introduced to the Seacoast Cancer Center and I must say it was a very pleasant experience and it completely changed my ideas of WDH because before that I had been in the old building. The hospital had expanded and was much more attractive." He joined the Board in 2006 and discovered the time commitment required to be on the Board came with a great deal of satisfaction and an expanded knowledge about health care. "We participate in two or three committees outside the Board that allows us to interact with more and more administrative and sometimes non-administrative members of the hospital. I think we are pretty well rounded as a Board. We also have physician voting board members who give us a broader perspective about what goes on in the hospital and the community."

The Garrison addition, planned for many years and originally as a five-story building, was designed to alleviate overcrowding in the hospital and prepare a place to care for the burgeoning baby boomer generation, as well as a booming baby trend. A bleak financial outlook at the end of 2008, since dubbed the Great Recession, delayed the project. CFO Peter Walcek recalled the insecurities of that time. "I thought that our business was almost recession proof. This one simply showed us that our business is not necessarily recession proof. Our volume dropped like a stone for the last two quarters of 2008 and the first couple of quarters for 2009, I recall it very vividly - that had never happened in my tenure or in any records I could find."

The hospital waited, watched the economy improve, and volume turn around. Architects adjusted the size and scope of the new building project; the hospital's "A" bond rating led to low interest rates and the $40 million construction project began in 2011. Walker said the new four-story addition was long overdue and the "only option to give us the space we need with the privacy, security, and comfort patients want and deserve."

Birthing room

Hannaford Special Care Nursery

C-Section OR

Women & Children's Center entrance

Garrison Wing Conference Center Lobby

Women & Children's Center lobby

Adult patient room

Garrison Wing, fourth floor

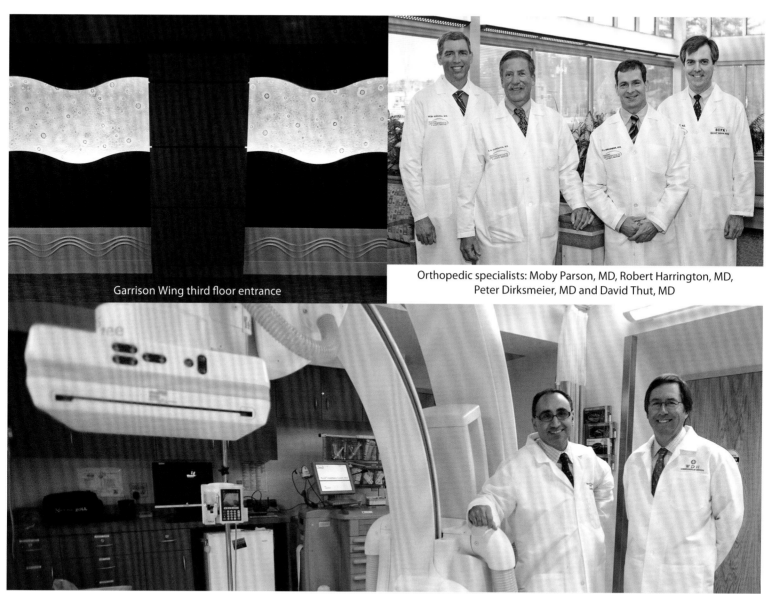

Garrison Wing third floor entrance

Orthopedic specialists: Moby Parson, MD, Robert Harrington, MD, Peter Dirksmeier, MD and David Thut, MD

Cardiologists: Lazaro Diaz, MD and William Danford, MD

Donna Smith, RN, Joint Replacement Program Coordinator

Trustee Janet Perry and friends at fundraising event

Seacoast Cancer Center 5K Walk/Run

Leslie Latimer, Pharmacy   John Gillespie, MD, OB/GYN   David Novis, MD, Pathology   Glenn Bacon, MD, Anesthesia

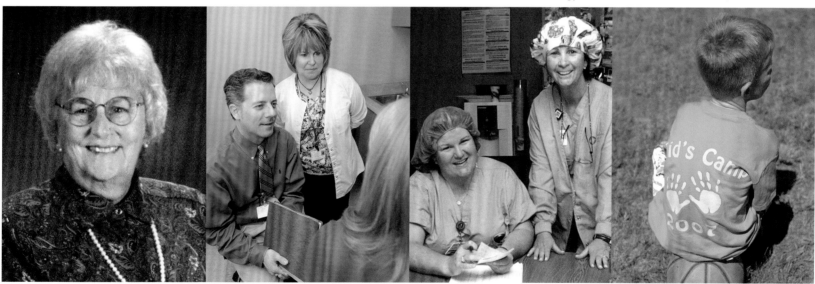

Ann Torr, Trustee   John Schorge, MD, GYN/Oncology and Kathleen Quinn, RN, Nurse Navigator   Joan Matthews, CNOR and Cindy Wyskiel, RN

79

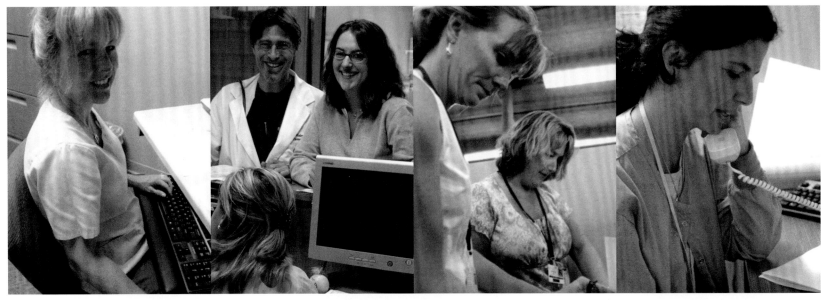

Sheila Woolley, RN, CNO and
VP of Patient Care Services

Roger Dionne
Environmental Services

Bill Irvine, HR

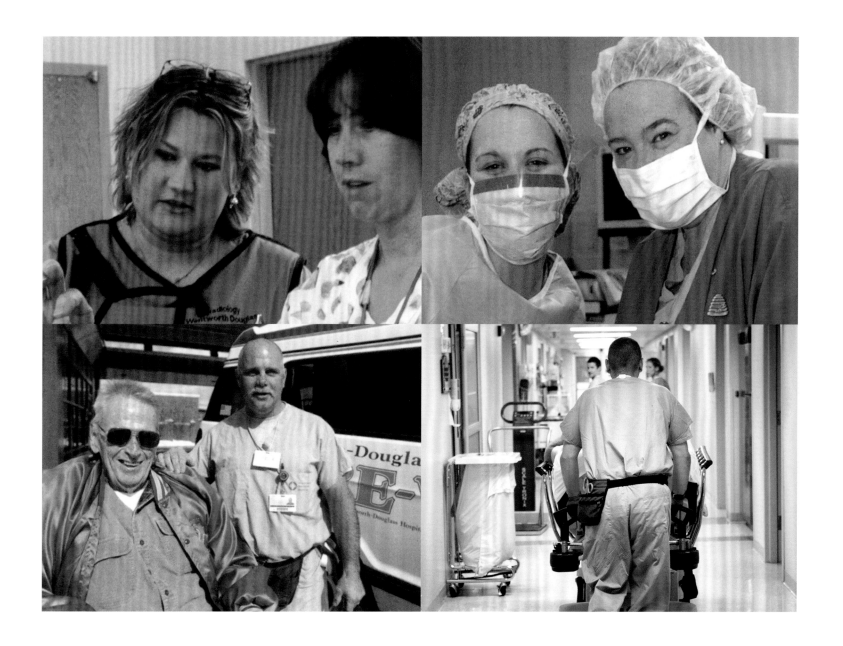

2006 Board of Trustees:
(l-r) back row: Malcolm McNeill, David Novis, MD, Wesley Kennedy, David Flavin, MD, Ann Torr, Ted Ristaino, Carol Bailey, Gregory Walker, Roger Hamel, Steve Webb, Michael Steinberg
front row: Wil Boc, Donna Rinaldi, Eugene Soares, MD, Tina Nadeau and Gerald Daley.

84

Gregory Walker, President & CEO of Wentworth-Douglass Health System, presents a $125,000 grant to fight opioid abuse to Anthony F. Colarusso, Jr., Chief of the Dover Police Department, and members of the Dover Youth to Youth Program and Dover Coalition for Youth.

Donors Maryann & Clayton Wentworth

Donors James and Frances Kageleiry

Donors Richard and Janet Conley

Donors Mike McClurken, PhD and Jackie Eastwood

Donors Tricia and Bob DeColfmacker

Garrison Wing fourth floor entrance

Chapter 15: Programmatic Advancements

In addition to multiple construction projects, the exponential growth of programs during this era occasionally elicited concern from the executive team, wishing at times growth would slow down. But, the very people who wanted relief from the intensity of work days were the same ones bringing in the new concepts. Walker smiled at the suggestion that workload might slow or stop some day at WDH. "It's like anything else, you hire really talented people and they give great ideas and nobody wants to stop. It's amazing."

One of the first ideas came to fruition in 2001 with the opening of the Wound Healing Institute that eventually moved to the lower level of the Ambulatory Building. Vascular surgeon Michael Southworth, MD, explained the purpose of the Wound Healing Institute in the hospital's annual report for 2001. "Wentworth-Douglass Hospital has opened a Wound Healing Institute to treat patients whose wounds won't heal normally due to diabetes, arterial disease, infection, trauma, and other medical conditions. Modern wound healing involves surgical cleaning of wounds and a team approach between doctors and nurses." By 2005, the center added an adjunctive service for the healing of complex wounds and brought Hyperbaric Oxygen (HBO) services on board with deep-dive healing technology.

Other programmatic innovations during the early century included the introduction of Integrative Therapies and Integrative Medicine, the opening of the Center for Medical Genetics, directed by Eugene R. Soares, MD, and the Sup- portive and Palliative Care Program, currently headed by Agata Marszalek Litauska, MD.

Hospitalists arrive

The Hospitalist Program was received with some reluctance when it was introduced in 2004 with only a few providers, a number that has since expanded to include 14 physicians and 3 nurse practitioners. John Novello, MD, President of the Medical Staff and a hospitalist, recognized the complexities of the program when he remarked, "Even I was skeptical as a physician that the Hospitalist Program would continue successfully here. I think the core group that started most of the practice were actually very good clinicians. They quickly gained the respect of the medical staff and it changed how medicine was practiced."

Hospitalized patients have the advantage of a group of providers who are available 24/7 at the hospital, freeing primary care physicians to see their office patients without the need to go back and forth to the hospital. "Hospitalists provide outstanding care in the inpatient setting and allow primary care providers more time to provide outstanding care to their patients in the outpatient setting."

Cardiology adds Vascular

Along with other expansions over the years, the Cardiovascular Program began with the Cardiology Department and a single catheterization lab in the early eighties. As the years passed, the hospital replaced old equipment with new, adding staff and expertise. The underpinnings of the newest Cardio-vascular Interventional Lab began at a Murder Mystery event in 2010. This fundraiser at The Governor's Inn in Rochester supported the purchase of equipment for a second, state-of-the-art Interventional Lab at WDH to provide faster access to patients in the grip of a cardiac event. The new Lab was also equipped to perform specialized vascular procedures. By 2012, Cardiology and Vascular Services came together, forming Wentworth Health Partners Cardiovascular Group. At the time, new team members explained the benefits of the combined effort. Cardiologist William Danford, MD, commended his new partner, vascular surgeon Robert Oram, MD, for his ability to do vein bypasses, commenting, "We can handle more complex patients now. It's like a mini Mayo Clinic here." Dr. Oram said it "just made sense." Both specialists treated the same disorders and crossed paths many times. "Cardiologists understand what I do and I understand what they do," Oram said. "I've always been a big believer in collaborative medicine and integrated systems." With the arrival of cardiologist, Lillian Joventino, MD, a specialist in abnormal heart rhythms, the group also added expertise in electrophysiology allowing patients with implanted cardiac devices to stay in their home community for care. Local businessman and cardiac arrest victim, Dennis Ciotti, praised the hospital's Cardiovascular Care Center and its staff in 2013 for being knowledgeable, kind and caring for him and his family. "They saved my life - I can't say enough."

**Musculoskeletal Health, Joint Replacement,
Spine Center, Rehab**
Baby boomers want it all - wellness advocates, diet experts,

skilled rehab therapists, and new joints when their originals wear out. The field of musculoskeletal health is thriving because Physical Medicine and Rehabilitation specialist Barry Gendron, DO, believes boomers "aren't willing to accept the aches and pains and limitations that perhaps their parents accepted because of their age." With 10,000 per day hitting retirement age, the baby boomer generation is spurring new programs and services unheard of even ten years ago. "I think people are getting smarter about training and know a lot more community resources are available." He noted how the hospital-owned Works Family Health & Fitness Center has recently expanded to include health coaches and its first dietician to create a collaborative, less expensive medical environment more focused on wellness.

As orthopedic surgeon Guy Esposito, MD, recognized early in his career at Wentworth-Douglass, joint replacement did not exist when he began in the seventies. An intense interest in the field led to a subspecialty focus on joint replacement and years later to a new Joint Replacement Center at Wentworth-Douglass. The center opened in 2007 to provide pre- and post-surgery group education and rehab then moved to the Garrison Wing. Orthopedic surgeon Moby Parsons, MD, said his practice became firmly committed to working with Wentworth-Douglass in achieving its goal of developing a joint replacement center. "This is truly a center of excellence." Dr. Parsons also developed an expertise in shoulder joint replacement and anterior hip replacement as the program grew. One of the program's patients summed up the value of the new program since she had her first knee replacement prior to its opening. "What a world of difference. I don't see

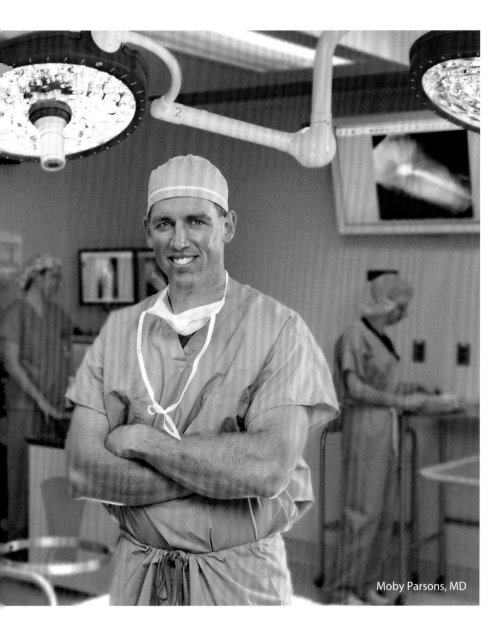

Moby Parsons, MD

how it can possibly get any easier for a person to get back on the road to recovery."

Another advancement in knee replacement has been the development of custom made implants based on 3D CT scans taken of the individual patient's knee preoperatively. "Each implant is unique to the patient's anatomy," Dr. Gendron explained. He also noted that between 1993, when he joined the medical staff, and today there is a greater reliance on aquatic therapy for joint patients and "the skill level of the physical therapists (PT) really changed." He believes the higher level of skill is the result of changes in training and the requirement for a doctorate. "The skill level of the PT has really changed; in '93 physical therapists couldn't do manipulation, now their practice acts have changed and they can do manipulation…they are coming out with more and more skills."

Targeted spine care was added to the musculoskeletal programs with the advent of The Northern New England Spine Center partnership, a virtual system coordinated through the WDH Rehabilitation Department and independent medical practices. It is a collaborative program involving a spine surgeon, physiatrists, anesthesiologists specializing in pain medicine, spine physical therapists, nutritionists, and specialists in pain psychology, and the "mind body connection". The program provides a streamlined approach to the care of the high volume of often complicated patients suffering with painful neck and back problems. Spine surgeon Peter Dirksmeier, MD, explained, "The Northern New England Spine Center offers a uniquely efficient and effective treatment approach to WDH patients. Mutually agreed upon treatment protocols and multidisciplinary patient care conferences provide prompt access to all appropriate providers thus maximizing patient experience and outcomes."

Musculoskeletal Health's Neuro Day Program encompasses new forms of care for patients suffering concussions by working with primary care providers and physical, occupational and speech therapists. "Nationally, concussion has really come to the forefront and patients are actually demanding attention. When they have a concussion they are concerned they are going to end up like the NFL players," Dr. Gendron said. At a recent concussion symposium at Wentworth-Douglass attended by over 100 providers, Dr. Gendron noted the focus was not only on care but on prevention. A speaker from UNH gave an overview of their efforts at "helmet-less" football training. "They practice without helmets so players learn not to spear, not to use their heads … we are seeing sports actually changing their way of practicing… it's quite interesting."

Pediatric rehabilitation is the next advance on the immediate horizon for Musculosketal Health services at WDH. This program will be a first of its kind for the hospital and a real benefit for the community.

Robotics

Guy Esposito, MD, chairman of Wentworth-Douglass Hospital's department of surgery in 2006, called robotic-assisted surgery a "big breakthrough" and Wentworth-Douglass was on the leading edge. "You can do everything you can do with open surgery and you can get to places you can't get with open surgery. It's a new tool that's allowing us to do better things for our patients."

In an article in 2009, GYN/Oncologist John Schorge, MD, Chief of Gynecological Oncology at Massachusetts General Hospital, explained his role in the newly formed clinical affiliation and GYN Oncology program at WDH. The program began in 2008 to bring advanced subspecialty care to the Seacoast to treat women with ovarian and other gynecologic cancers. A surgeon with many skills, Dr. Schorge uses the daVinci robotic surgical system to "reduce the size of surgical incisions and help patients recover quickly." He works closely with the team of OB/GYN surgeons on staff at WDH to provide care in the local community when appropriate. Dr. Schorge said, "The OB/GYN group here is terrific. They're a cohesive group and excellent surgeons. Patients don't really want to go to Boston, so I'm glad I can come here. Patients are getting great care."

In a recent interview, urologist Dr. Roger Evans, MD, said among the hospital's strengths are the skill of the medical staff and "a good armamentarium of treatments" developed over time including robotic surgery. Its early uses were in the field of urology and gynecology but today, he noted, "the bulk of cases now are general surgery" for gall bladder, colon and even some hernia surgery."

Community Benefit: A Helping Hand

Community service has been part of Wentworth-Douglass Hospital's substance since its early days, caring for those who could not pay, educating the public about ways to better

Jessica Crane, surgical tech trainer and John Schorge, MD

health, and creating transportation solutions to ease the burden of getting care - long before the State of NH and the federal government required filings under the heading of "Community Benefit."

Millions of dollars, supported in part by generous donors, are annually allotted to community benefit programs; the early years of this century are ripe with these efforts at WDH. Financial assistance, medication assistance, and the Care-Van Free Patient Transport program were among the first to be supported by the Board of Trustees as the new century took hold. The Care-Van program expanded from a limited service for Seacoast Cancer Center patients to a broader program for eligible patients receiving treatments in other hospital departments. The hospital also collaborated, at a later date, with Dover Housing Authority to develop the *Hand in Hand* transportation program for their residents.

In 2005, Community Benefit funds supported the opening of Wentworth-Douglass Community Dental Center for low income adults and children and garnered additional support from local business and community members. By 2014, the Board's emphasis moved to the troubling issues surrounding behavioral health identified in a community survey. While agreeing to continue established programs, they also approved funding to provide behavioral health services in primary care practices and to augment assistance in the Emergency Department. Kellie Mueller, M.Ed, Director of Social Work and Behavior Health Services, said at the time that feeling better for some patients may not only include medical exams, diagnostic tests, or prescriptive care, but that it

also involves paying attention to their emotional health. "We have developed a program that brings licensed clinical social workers out of their traditional setting to the primary care office location – making for a more collaborative connection that is seamless and more comforting for our patients."

WDH hopes its recent effort to collaborate with Frisbie Memorial Hospital will bring the hospitals and the state together to find solutions to the drug and opioid problem facing NH and the nation. President Walker told a gathering of community leaders in November 2015, this project has to be a county wide-effort, adding the hospital boards are working together through a broader community benefit process to "find funding and resources" to prevent the tragic losses from overdoses in their communities.

Part 4: Spanning the Decades

Within the history of Wentworth-Douglass Hospital key programs have crossed multiple decades from their early beginnings to the current day. Here are their stories.

Chapter 16: Nursing and Care Teams

Grace Haskell was a nurse who taught nurses and taught them well. Even years after her death, nursing students followed her strict rules while learning the art and science of caring for patients. While the basics stayed the same through the decades the tasks and responsibilities expanded year by year.

In the years Ruth Griffin worked as a nursing student between 1943 and 1946, she cared for a woman suffering from bone cancer who was a patient for the entire three years. "She used to get a quarter of a grain of morphine, subcutaneous, every six hours around the clock. She had such excruciating pain, but she lived a long time because we took such good care of her. I think a lot of my success in my life had a start there. I certainly got a good work ethic."

In the sixties Administrator Vince DeNobile noted the changing role of nursing and introduced the concept of a team of caregivers working together in a period of "increasing complexity of patient care." He explained, "The role of the nurse has expanded dramatically to encompass important, independent functions. Additional health team workers have joined her in a nursing team to assist in carrying out the doctor's orders in conjunction with a plan for nursing care."

Nursing in the seventies increased its professional scope to meet the demands of new technologies and new services. Director of Nursing Services at the time, Mary Ann Peters, RN, met with the Board of Trustees in 1976 to discuss her

WDH Nurses: (l-r) Paula Dresser, Fran Whiting, Doris Noyes and Beth Hutchinson

plans to expand the nursing program. Mrs. Peters told the trustees every nursing unit was in the process of examining the way nursing care was provided to improve patient care. "Rather than looking at the numbers of patients per nurse on any given floor, we are now looking at the needs of the patient." The Nursing Director noted some diseases required more nursing care than others. Her goal was to decentralize the management of the nursing department, allowing more

97

decision making to take place at lower management levels.

During the eighties, the nursing division went through more change. Former Assistant Director of Nursing Doris Noyes, RN, recalled working with the Director of Nursing Jim Mullen. "He was always making organizational changes. I was head nurse on Dunaway 2 for two years, then I became Assistant Director along with Agnes Rexroad - she was the other Assistant Director. When I came here we were still a small hospital, I felt like it was possible to know everybody and it was a great feeling - I loved that."

Even though Mullen hired Doris, Agnes Rexroad took the credit throughout her 30 plus years at WDH. Interviewed for the 1988 annual report, Mrs. Rexroad said she was hired the same day she sat down for an interview with Mary Ann Peters soon after she moved to Somersworth. As a mother of six daughters, her early career was spent working nights in Emergency and caring for her family during the day. She later served as Head Nurse on the Dunaway 2 inpatient unit, day supervisor, Assistant Director of Nursing,

Agnes Rexroad, RN

and eventually she became the first Patient Representative before retiring. "Ask Agnes" were two words most staff and physicians knew would get answers to almost any question. Always modest and soft spoken, she said at the time, "I am especially proud to be a member of the nursing staff at WDH and to live in this community - both have been very good to me."

Years later, CNO Sheila Woolley, RN, commented on the 1976 statement made by Nursing Director Mary Ann Peters, noting it was made the year Sheila graduated from nursing school. "I love what she said, it is so true today." She explained the education and development of nursing as a true profession has been a catalyst for some of the changes in nursing. "I think what is fascinating today, is that it has almost come full circle when they were caring for populations, as we are today, not necessarily curing diseases but helping people live well." Patient Care Services also developed a model for shared governance "that was a big change." "It's been great to see staff empowered and engaged at all levels - not just nursing but teams of caregivers working together to give the best care possible."

Chapter 17: Emergency Medicine

While the hospital took care of accident victims and emergency patients from its beginning days, the specialization of emergency medicine was still in its formative years well into the seventies. The hospital's Emergency Department (ED) was a constant source of local news material and evidence of a growing and vital community service. During this time period, a *Foster's* news story elaborated on a young man's life-threatening accident on the Garrison Hill's ski slope. The 16-year old patient recalled the event. "I must have crossed my skis and fell on my pole," he said. The jagged end punctured his wind pipe, plunged into his thyroid gland and tore open an artery. A rescue sled was hurried to the scene and dragged him down to the ED where John Stram, MD, met him. Dr. Stram told the reporter, "Five more minutes and he would have been dead." He believed the consistent mock disasters played out annually at the hospital were one reason the entire system worked so well and so quickly on that day explaining, "This was a real disaster and a real dead person would have come out of this. But he didn't."

Former Emergency Department Director Babu "Ram" Ramdev, MD, recently shared his memories of his earliest days at

Babu Ramdev, MD

the hospital. Unlike his colleagues in the hectic environment of an ED, Ram always looked like he could have graced the cover of GQ magazine. Every hair was in place and he wore dark suits, crisp shirts and silk ties. Even though he has retired, he serves on the Hospital's Foundation Board and looks the same today with a few more grey hairs and has just as much enthusiasm for medicine as he had when he began.

As a surgeon trained in England, and doing research in Western Ontario, he said he had no intention of becoming an emergency physician in 1976. During a visit to family in NH, a physician friend enticed Dr. Ramdev to consider moving his family to the Seacoast and suggested he contact the hospital in Dover that was looking for someone to run emergency. Soon after, he accepted the position, joining Peter Bradley, MD, in a small, three-room setting at the back of the hospital. Not yet a 24/7 service, they saw 10,000 patients a year supported by physicians from the entire medical staff, regardless of their specialties. Dr. Ramdev explained how services worked at the time. "The hospital by-laws said every physician had to take night call - Bill Cusack (OB/GYN), Colokathis, Jack Myers, Roger Temple, Pat Adams… they all did night calls. If somebody didn't want to come in they had to pay $100." Paul Young (pathologist), Ram laughed, "he paid the $100." What was fascinating, he added, "When non-emergency physicians did night call no one got sued … it wasn't even their field." The group expanded to four and more as years passed, now serving over 50,000 patients a year.

One of the greatest advances in emergency care happened outside the hospital. Dr. Ramdev highlighted the important role played by pre-hospital caregivers. "We had EMTs in the seventies and paramedics came in the eighties who played a significant role in saving cardiac patients. The patient's EKG came in even before the patient came in. They made such a difference."

President Walker believes Emergency is the "front door" of the hospital. "When you look at the number of people that come through … the reputation of the hospital, to a great extent, is made from the experience people have in our Emergency Department. We know people drive past other hospitals to come here."

On very busy days, patients arrive every 8 to 12 minutes. In a 2011 interview, Nurse Director Ann Lak, RN, expressed her pride in the staff and described them as "problem solvers" who were extremely versatile and great patient advocates. At the same time Emergency Nurse Manager Stacey Savage, RN, now Nurse Director of the ED, said the ED can be the best and the worst place to work all at the same time. "We're exposed to horrible things every single day – no human should see a child die or watch a young man suffer severe pain from cancer. It's hard to go home and walk away some days." When patient volume and acuity are high the entire hospital responds. The speed and unexpected nature of the ED creates a rapid yet fluid response. "It's almost like choreographing a dance," Stacey said. "Everyone knows their part and the faster the pace the more we seem to move together. I think our nurses, doctors and the entire team stand out from any other hospital. They're really exceptional."

Emergency Medical Director Lukas Kolm, MD, a former UNH student and Durham ambulance driver took up the mantel of leadership after his mentor, Dr. Ramdev, retired. He said his team's persistence at quality and "passion for excellence" made him proud to be affiliated with the hospital. His role as an emergency doctor at the front lines of opiate abuse and his strong opinions as a leader in the NH Medical Society "made waves" in the fall of 2015 when he suggested the state's drug czar could do more. In a 2016 news story featuring Dr. Kolm as *Foster's Newsmaker of the Year*, the reporter described Dr. Kolm as "an energetic man who speaks in rapid, passionate bursts" and noted he " ignited a much-needed debate across New Hampshire about the opiate epidemic, which has claimed nearly 350 lives this year." The story continued to describe an incident when Dr. Kolm helped care for a man overdosing in the back of an American Ambulance in Somersworth. "He was blue and breathless," Dr. Kolm said. They administered a dose of naloxone, which reversed the effects of the opiate overdose. "That's what brought him back." Dr. Kolm said he plans to continue talking about opiates and addiction because the problem is "not going to fade away."

Chapter 18: Surgery

In the mid-19th century, physicians performed surgery in open operating theaters wearing an apron over their street clothes. Many were general practitioners (GPs). They used bare hands and unsterilized instruments and, until the 1840s, patients did not have anesthesia. By the early 20th century physicians began to specialize in medicine or surgery, each tract becoming more separate as the century moved on. They also began wearing gowns, however, several years elapsed before they consistently used caps, masks, and, finally, gloves.

Wentworth Hospital listed four attending physicians and four surgeons on staff in 1906. The medical staff doubled by the forties with 13 physicians in general practice and 2 eye, ear, nose and throat specialists Tom Reid, MD and John Hunter, MD. Dr. Marcotte was the radiologist. GPs did most of the work specialists do today. As Dr. Galt said, his practice included OB/GYN, surgery, orthopedics, and pediatrics. "I was chief of surgery for a number of years…we did it all back then." In a similar recollection Dr. Lampesis said that "consultants came up from Boston to do stomach surgery or brain surgery in an emergency or the patients were sent to Boston. Urologists came from Concord several times a week and then Bob Hatch, MD came in to do OB/GYN. I did anesthesia for about five years until it just got too busy."

Looking back, orthopedic surgeon Guy Esposito, MD, said he was amazed at the advances in his field of orthopedics since he joined Drs. DiMambro, Demopoulas, and Vittands in a

Doctor's Park office in the seventies. "Everything that is done today in orthopedic surgery, except setting bones and common fractures, didn't exist then. Total hips and total knees were just starting," he remarked, adding, "between '75 and '95 knowledge just exploded."

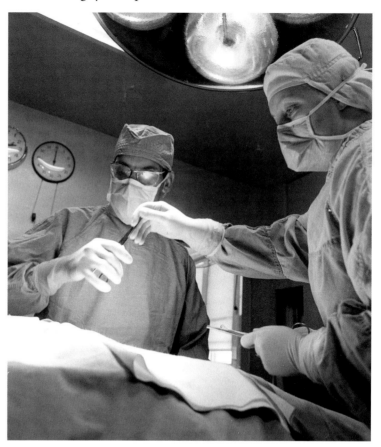

Guy Esposito, MD and Robert Harrington, MD

Long, open incisions and long hospital stays were soon replaced with new techniques that allowed surgery to be same-day events. The hospital's expertise in outpatient surgery was reviewed in an early eighties news article entitled, "Outpatient surgery becoming the 'in' thing." The article described a patient arriving for knee surgery at 6 a.m. and leaving for his home in South Berwick, Maine by 4 p.m. A procedure at the hospital known as arthroscopic surgery made the outpatient stay possible. John Bloom, MD, and Guy Esposito, MD, told the reporter they had been using arthroscopic surgery for about three years to assess the damage done to cartilage and tendons in the knee. Its surgical application made "people better quicker," Dr. Esposito said. "We get patients coming in earlier for surgery instead of limping around for days and doing permanent damage." Prior to arthroscopic surgery the patient would have had an open incision, would have stayed in the hospital for three days or more, and "perhaps be condemned to six weeks in a cast and prolonged rehabilitation."

Surgical scope procedures expanded beyond orthopedics and urology to the general surgery arena in the early nineties. General surgeon Paul Butler, MD, said at the time that a new procedure, called laparoscopic cholecystectomy, was in great demand by patients who suffered from gall bladder disease. The entire general surgery service, including H. Jack Myers, MD and Roger Temple, MD also performed this new procedure. Dr. Butler noted, "Prior to this, a patient would have a long incision, spend 4-5 days in the hospital recovering and 4-6 weeks after that away from work and family responsibilities." Thanks to this new technology many patients were home in 24-36 hours with very little discomfort and returned to full activities "in just seven days."

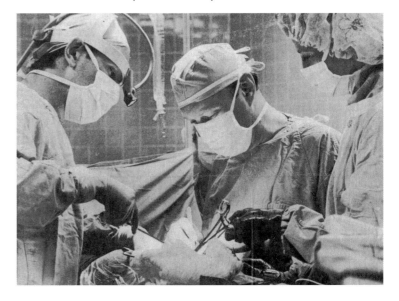

The outpatient surgery program escalated at WDH as more and more surgical specialties adopted minimally invasive procedures. Roger Evans, MD, current chief of surgery, noted two areas that led to significant changes since his arrival in 1978 as a urologist working in Dr. John Lanni's group. The first was a change in philosophy and anesthesia. "Ambulatory surgery evolved because of a better understanding of the healing process and better anesthetic agents, so patients didn't have a lot of postoperative nausea. The second change was more technical. Scientific advancements (scope procedures) gave us the ability to be much more minimally invasive. There was no wound to get infected, less pain. Beyond my specialty, each of the other specialties have had similar advancements."

Anesthesia

As Dr. Evans noted, anesthesia played an important role in the advent of outpatient surgery. James McKenna, MD, arrived in 1986, one of the first group of board certified, residency trained anesthesiologists. Before his time, as Dr. Lampesis and Dr. Galt recalled, anesthesia was done by general practitioners. "It was a little like the dark ages in the late seventies, early eighties when family docs were doing anesthesia - but that was the way it was then. When surgical specialists came along like (Dr.) John Stram (ear, nose and throat surgeon), they realized the hospital wouldn't go anywhere without trained anesthesiologists. Plus other docs like Ingvar Vittands (orthopedic surgeon) wanted real anesthesiologists. That's when (Dr.) John Schermerhorn and (Dr.) Bob Andleman came, docs who did their training and residency in anesthesiology. Surgery was getting more complex, we had

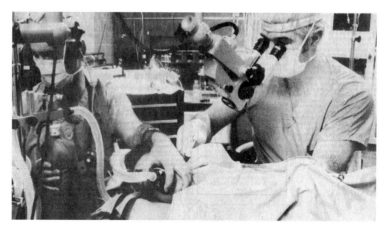

new and better drugs. Patients could go home without side effects. We had nerve blocks and patients woke up quicker.

"Older drugs like ether made people sick. Now we have drugs with no side effects that are so superior to what we used years ago. We routinely use anti-emetic or anti-nausea drugs, originally developed for cancer patients, to prevent nausea. One of the newest drugs used in joint surgery patients is an ultra long acting local anesthetic that can last up to three days. These drugs enable patients with major surgeries, joints, shoulder surgery, to go home the same day. In the next five years we think most patients will be pain free and most will go home the same day even from major procedures."

Looking Inside

The first X-ray department at Wentworth Hospital opened in 1918, followed by an upgrade in 1925, the year the hospital was granted Class A ranking by the American Hospital Association. In a speech years later to the Dover Rotary Club at the Sterling Motel on "Advances in Modern Medicine," Bernard Manning, MD, described the hospital in 1931, noting at the time that Dr. Chesley "developed his own plates in his one man X-ray laboratory." The department expanded over the years, adding a darkroom and angiography equipment in 1977, described by radiologist Bernard Casey, MD, as a "new piece of equipment which will enable the staff to locate the point of internal bleeding, obstructions, narrowing of veins and arteries, and other related ailments."

By 1986 the Radiology Department's services included the region's first CT scanner and in the same year opened a mobile mammography service in a joint venture with Frisbie Memorial Hospital that would become Women's Life Imaging Center, in Somersworth, NH. By 2003, the first fixed MRI arrived at Wentworth-Douglass followed by full digital imaging, and the Radiology Department became known as Imaging Services.

Imaging's current department chair, Shannon Nedelka, MD, of Seacoast Radiology, PA, described imaging advancements as years of just X-ray and film to a period of remarkable change in diagnostic capabilities. "We can see inside the body - it's really kind of miraculous and we don't have to invade the body in any way," she said. "For many years we had X-ray and then we added barium to see soft tissue - we could see things never seen by X-ray before. Tomography took the X-ray another step - taking slices of pictures…giving greater detail to specific organs of the body."

By the nineties image guided systems were being used in minimally invasive surgery and interventional radiologists performed procedures to open blocked blood vessels. From 2002 on, WDH has produced digital images and is a completely filmless service today. "Our primary care providers can log into the WDH system with its HIPAA privacy protections and see images, read our notes, and they can show their patients the images too. We can also do 3D reconstruction of body parts to assist surgeons with their surgical planning and non-invasive colon imaging for use as a primary diagnostic tool."

The department added low-dose CT scanning as part of a structured Lung Cancer Screening program in 2015 in an effort to find and treat lung cancers at earlier stages. Wentworth Health Partners physicians work closely with their patients in the program to provide counseling and smoking cessation programs while "patients come in annually for screenings just like a mammogram." A nurse from the hospital's Chest Clinic coordinates the screenings and followup care. CT imaging is also a vital component of the hospital's stroke program, producing images as quickly as possible to help Emergency Department physicians and neurologists determine the most appropriate treatment to stop or prevent further brain damage.

Advances in imaging services have also led to improvements in exposure to radiation. "The new imaging systems produce decreased doses of radiation while maintaining quality images," Dr. Nedelka explained. "The CTs of today compared to those of the late seventies and early eighties have approximately 20 times less radiation. It will just continue to get better."

Chapter 19: Babies

Dover resident and current hospital volunteer Ann Herlihy, a petite woman with a pixie haircut and face to match, delivered her first baby boy at the Wentworth Hospital just before the '54 building and new maternity department opened. The unit was in the Administration Building on the second floor in the back. Patients labored in one room and were wheeled across the hall to the one delivery room. The nursery was on the first floor, down the stairs. Her family doctor, Peter Lampesis, MD, delivered all her boys. "I had four babies in three and one half years and I had the longest continuous diaper service of anyone - seven years," she laughed. "They didn't have Pampers back then."

Ann Herlihy, Volunteer

Dr. Jesse Galt, another GP who delivered babies in the mid-fifties, recalled his days going up and down stairs. "If a C-section was necessary, second floor patients had to be carried on a stretcher down a winding stairway. In some areas there were bare wires running across the ceiling." Just like many departments in the hospital, maternity services expanded and moved when space opened up. By 1978, borning rooms, later called birthing rooms, arrived at the hospital, moving a traditional design into a more contemporary setting. The borning room was described as an "alternative" that continued to offer the safety of a hospital birth in a home-like setting. OB/GYN William Cusack, Jr, MD, chief of staff at Wentworth-Douglass at the time, described the first borning rooms as more home-like where "long blue-flowered curtains" concealed "an incubator, instrument table, oxygen and suction apparatus, and all that other unfriendly - looking stuff, unfriendly but necessary."

William Cusack, MD

Another change in the birthing methods at WDH, midwifery, would become a centerpiece of the hospital's obstetrical services from the mid-seventies to the present day. Certified Nurse Midwife Judy Edwards, NH's first midwife, elaborated

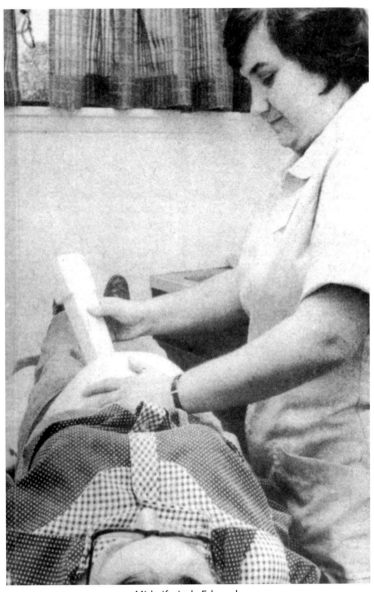
Midwife Judy Edwards

on her role in the delivery process for a news story in 1975. Midwives, working only in a hospital setting, Ms. Edwards remarked, were a "super idea" for the general population since "most births are normal." It was a good alternative, she believed, for women who "aren't into home birth." She also emphasized the quality already available for all types of births at the hospital, rating it as "excellent" with "good communication with fathers." "Nothing is rigid about the birthing process," she said, explaining the lengths she would go to help moms deliver. The reporter noted, "Although it might take her a few minutes to figure out how to handle it, she (Ms. Edwards) would probably allow a woman to deliver on her hands and knees if she wanted to."

Director of Maternal Child Karen MacDonald, RN, began in 1986 as the nursery manager before the hospital combined the maternity unit and the nursery and, later, added pediatrics. She recalled working with Jeannine Towle, RN, the maternity nurse manager who was one of the last graduates of the hospital's nursing school. Miss Towle never had children of her own but she made new moms feel like she had several. The main entrance to the hospital was still facing Central Avenue when MacDonald began; a month later the new wing opened. "I got to see the old and be part of the new."

Why do moms choose WDH?
In the early 20th century it was rare to have a hospital delivery; only about one percent of babies were born at the Wentworth Hospital in its early years. Today, it is equally as rare to have an at-home delivery. MacDonald described the new center that opened in the Garrison Wing in 2013 with all

private rooms that serve as a single location for labor, delivery, recovery, and brief postpartum (LDRP) stays. "Now we have LDRPs, partners stay, we have refrigerators in rooms, and large spaces for families to visit." A recent market survey gave high marks to the Garrison Wing facility as "a definite plus" and staff as "very competent." MacDonald explained, "Our staff give personalized, individualized, compassionate care, and we have very competent doctors. If patients want a natural delivery, providers are "very supportive and it is all about choice."

Janet Perkins, MD, OB/GYN and chair of the OB Department, said she still cries every time a baby is born and believes "there is still a lot of mystery to birth and part of me hopes that never goes away." When she counsels a pregnant woman in her office who asks how the birthing process will go, Dr. Perkins tells her, "I really have to let you in on a little secret. I don't often need to be there. I am just standing by. Your body knows what to do and we should let it. There are very few times in a birth when you want me and when you do want me, you really want me. I can respond to things like hemorrhage, hypertensive disorder, eclampsia, but there are very few OB emergencies. I feel privileged to be part of the birthing process. It's a very intimate part a woman's life."

Creating the most natural birthing process is one of the reasons moms from a wide area of the Seacoast choose to deliver at WDH. Dr. Perkins promises her patients "we will try really hard to make this as much like a home birth as possible. Our nurses are like doulas, they are so awesome - we get birth, we are here for women, we have each other's backs. We can even

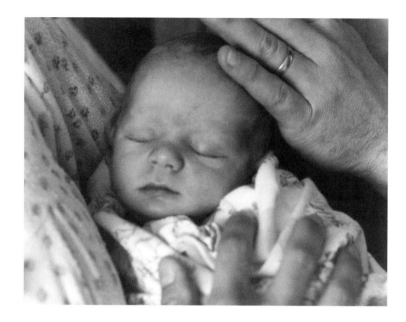

recreate a natural birth process in the C-section room. We've been doing this for years. I make my incisions really small so the baby's head gets squeezed through the birth canal to get rid of secretions and we do skin to skin right away. We dim the lights, play music. Mom can see her baby coming up…not missing a beat. We begin breastfeeding right away. This really is the place to deliver."

Breastfeeding has cycled in an out of popularity over the decades. Before and up to the mid-twentieth century, most moms breastfed their babies. By the 1950s, with the advent of new brands of bottles and formula, MacDonald noted "breastfeeding was no longer in vogue, modern women didn't want to breastfeed." During that period an estimated 80% of

American mothers used bottles. The bottle had displaced the breast. By the 1980s the trend reversed and now over 80% of moms breastfeed their babies. Wentworth-Douglass Hospital's focus on the importance of breastfeeding, and its high breastfeeding rate, earned the center designation as Baby Friendly in 2014.

Fatherhood has changed with the times too. Ms. MacDonald noted that years ago, fathers were not involved in the labor or delivery process. "Back then fathers did not help, now fathers think it's their delivery too." She believes father involvement is ideal. "It's great that dads are so involved, they're awesome."

For the past several years, the Women & Children's Center has led the Seacoast area in birthing volume. It was not always that busy, but its reputation, and location in the fastest growing area in NH, may attribute to its burgeoning births. Since his arrival in 1997, President Walker noted the hospital has more than doubled birth numbers from just over 500 that year to 1163 babies in 2015. "It's an amazing change, half of our births come from our primary service area, the other are from towns and cities outside of that."

Pediatrician Terri Lally, MD, believes the new Women & Children's Center design is a "big plus" for parents seeking a birth center. "A birth can happen in a warm, spacious, inviting space with as little or as much medical support/technology as is required. I think the quality, caring, passion, and commitment of providers has been a constant in the years I've been here."

Pediatrics
Pediatric inpatient units have all but vanished from most community hospitals thanks to medications and immunizations preventing many of the major childhood diseases. Dr. Lally believes Dover Pediatrics has evolved over the years to provide excellent care for the community's children. "We added three new pediatricians and two new nurse practitioners in the last few years. It's great to have these strong

WDH pediatricians welcome Dartmouth Hitchcock Medical Center's neonatologist George Little, MD, to the new Perinatal Program for Advanced Intensive Care at WDH. (l-r) Leonard Small, MD, Andre Vanderzanden, MD, Dr. Little, Patricia Adams, MD, nusery head nurse Karen MacDonald and Eugene Soares, MD.

new providers continue the high quality pediatric care at WDH that started with Dr. Wilson and was passed down through those former Dover Pediatrics doctors - Drs. Rockenmacher, Vanderzanden, Adams, Small, and Soares - who all gave so much to this community."

One of the pediatricians mentioned by Dr. Lally was Patricia Adams, MD. In an interview in 1973 about the size and scope of pediatric services at Wentworth-Douglass Hospital, Dr. Adams emphasized the extraordinary quality of care available. "We have, from time to time, significantly ill patients, children suffering from leukemia and viral pneumonia, for example. Some very sick children are sent to Boston, but many are cared for in the Dover hospital. The hospital's nursing staff is excellent. Something I really enjoy are the nurses on the floor…they're good and they're a lot of fun."

The life of a pediatrician was filled with challenging demands, not the least of which was on-call duty. Noting the extraordinary number of hours, sometimes entire nights Dr. Adams spent on-call in the Emergency Department, Dr. Ramdev once asked her how she was able to cope with such demands placed upon her. She answered, "I regard my patients as children of my own and I'm here to help them." Dr. Adams excelled in her career, serving as a trustee and President of the Medical Staff, receiving accolades from the New Hampshire Pediatric Society for her contributions to community, regional, and state pediatric causes. An endowment in her name was established in 2014 by her beloved husband, Robert Adams, to "perpetuate her love of children and concern for their families" and to " support programs offered

Robert Wilson, MD and Jeannine Towle, RN, Maternity, with new mom and infant

by the hospital and other entities that enhance the quality of life of children, particularly those with special needs." After suffering many years from Alzheimer's disease, Dr. Adams passed away in 2015.

Dana St. Laurent RN, Manager of the Women & Children's Center, also recalled WDH in the seventies when she started. "It was seven rooms, with up to four cribs in a room. Parents did not stay back then, care was so different. We used those bubble tops and croup tents; they were horrible, plastic tents and cool mist would come out, but they did work. We had a lot of children with asthma before they had treatments they could do at home. Kids would come in just coughing and be admitted. We took care of surgical patients. Appendectomies and tonsillectomies stayed about seven days. Parents would drop off their kids to have their tonsils out and pick them up in a week."

Pediatric volume is less today, but the kids that do get admitted are sicker. The care is more focused as well, thanks to the Dover Pediatric group working as hospitalists - "that's been a really great change," Dana added. Today's parents are also more involved in the care of their children, thanks to the vast amount of information available on-line. Dr. Lally said parents and patients have much more information to process and they want to be more knowledgeable and informed. "I've often told parents that pediatricians spend ninety percent of

their time educating and only ten percent of the time actually fixing something. So the information explosion, I think has offered both challenges and resources."

Dr. Perkins also described the Dover Pediatric group as "amazing" and she is grateful for their expertise caring for newborns, especially babies of addicted moms, born dependent on narcotics. "They are really good at it and deserve a lot of credit." Approximately three percent of babies born at Wentworth-Douglass Hospital suffer from Neonatal Abstinence Syndrome requiring extra care as they are weaned from dependency. Volunteer cuddlers are also available to bring comfort to these little ones.

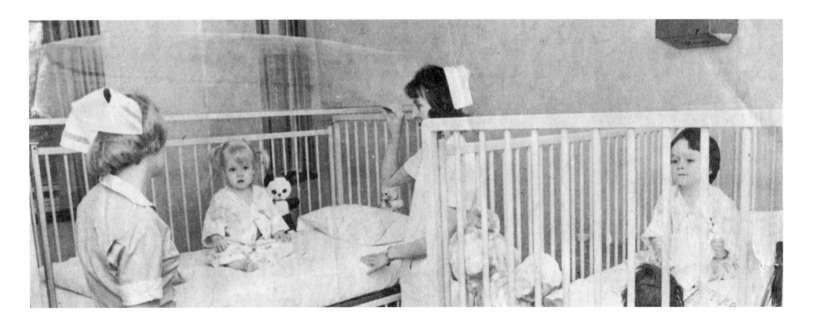

Chapter 20: Cancer Care

The roots of what would become the Seacoast Cancer Center, a regional oncology program that grew exponentially over the past 37 years, began humbly in two small rooms at the back of the Emergency Department in August 1979. The waiting room featured hard, plastic molded chairs in seventies colors of olive green and harvest gold, ganged along the edges of walls, atop grey linoleum floors. Vending machines for candy and cigarettes lined the entryway. The smell of tobacco smoke filled the air and spent butts lay in ash receptacles. It is hard to imagine the scene where cancer patients once waited for care. On a recent day in 2015, Dr. Sonneborn took a break between patient visits in the Seacoast Cancer Center to go back in time to a place where he and Lou Michaud, RN, began oncology services.

"Lou and I mixed all the chemotherapy. She and I started all the IVs and then when people were done, she booked their appointments, their X-rays, she did everything. We started one or two days then quickly expanded as it got busier and busier and more sophisticated. Then Bill Richwagen got the CON (certificate of need) for the radiation unit. After radiation came, the program just took off. We were all over the hospital in many different locations. The last clinic was on the third floor. We had four exam rooms. We really loved it there and then we moved here (Seacoast Cancer Center) in 1993. It just got better and better."

Radiation oncologist Asa Nixon, MD, has worked closely with Dr. Sonneborn and his colleagues since he came to the Seacoast Cancer Center in 1999, not sure at first he had found the right place. "When I got here I was looking for a hospital - a bigger place. I was used to Boston hospitals. The hospital was a lot flatter then; it didn't have the new lobby with the waterfall yet. I was really struck and thought, oh my goodness, this is the hospi-

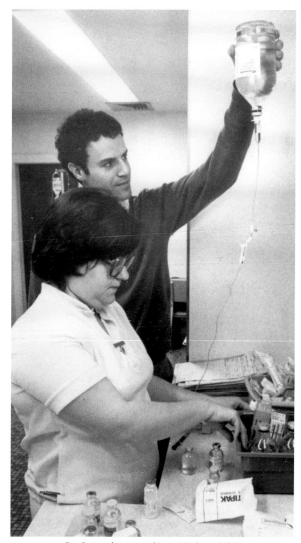

Dr. Sonneborn and Lou Michaud, RN

tal?" He stayed because a hospital is really more than a building. "We bring Boston quality up here so people don't have to go there. I enjoy coming up. This is much more of a community. The patients are great. I have long standing relationships with some of the patients. I've been here long enough so I already know the patient or someone related to a patient I've treated."

Asa Nixon, MD

The Seacoast Cancer Center is unique among hospitals in the region with radiation and medical oncology in the same center. Dr. Nixon said, "About five to ten times a day I'm running over to medical oncology or Henry (Sonneborn) is coming here. One of the biggest differences in cancer care over the past two decades is the multidisciplinary approach to lung cancer, head and neck cancer, gastro cancer, and brain tumors. When we are treating definitively for cure, we are using a combination of chemo and radiation therapy and sometimes surgery - it's not one or the other, but to be in a place where we are one unit is great for our patients."

High dose bracytherapy and IMRT moved into the Center in the first years of the new century followed in 2008 by a "quantum leap" in cancer treatment services. That year, a $9.3 million project introduced stereotactic radio surgery, using the Novalis TX accelerator to pinpoint the exact location of cancerous tumors. Its high energy radiation annihilated tumors that could not be reached by surgical procedures. The project included a second system, to provide additional treatment time and backup when system maintenance took place - a system and redundancy unheard of in a community hospital setting.

Dr. Sonneborn emphasized that cancer treatment is saving lives, and the Seacoast Cancer Center is at the forefront in both arenas - radiation and medical oncology therapies. Medications to treat cancer are expanding dramatically. "Today we're specifically targeting cancers. We have very effective nausea medications that we didn't have years ago. We seem to be curing more cancers and picking up cancers earlier. Smoking cessation has had a major impact, so have colonoscopies; we see early colon cancers…mammography has been revolutionary."

The hospital has added more screenings and specialists to identify and treat cancer. The recent introduction of low dose CT screening detects early lung cancers, and its treatment options expanded when the hospital affiliated with Massachusetts General Hospital. Dr. Nixon said the addition of specialists from Mass General, such as John Schorge, MD, and James Allen, MD, has enhanced the center's ability to care for even complex patients without the need to send them

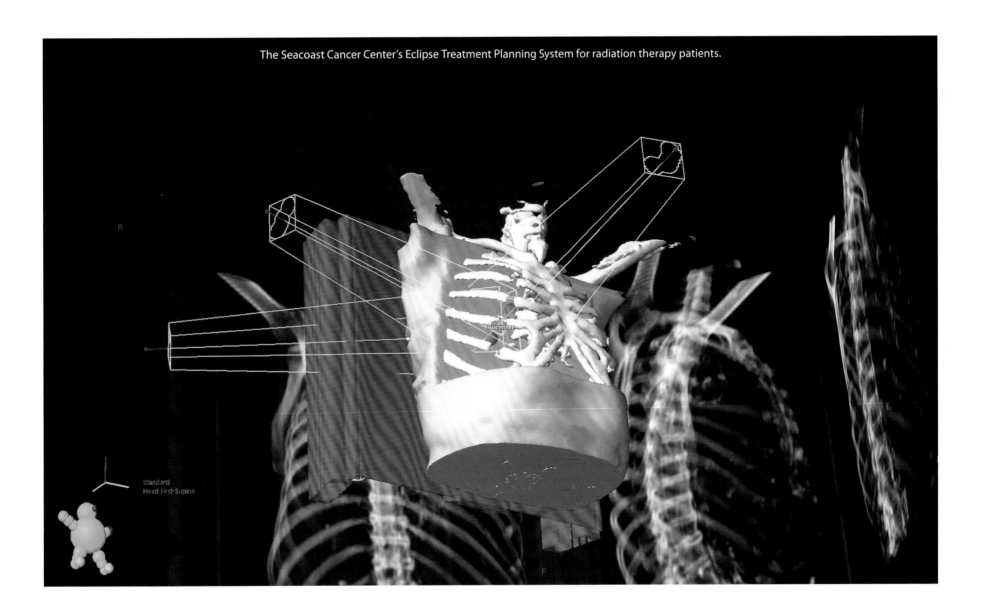

The Seacoast Cancer Center's Eclipse Treatment Planning System for radiation therapy patients.

the trials range from managing symptoms and improving quality of life to treatments with investigational medications and/or radiation."

President Walker attributed the cancer center's success to technology and new treatment modalities but he adds an important distinction, 'It's the people who work there, the credentials of the people working there are just phenomenal. We're really lucky." As the hospital's reputation spreads across New England, he remarked how easy it is to recruit some of the best physicians and key staff. "It's a great place to live. As you recruit some of these high caliber doctors, they tell their friends, then they want to come up here and it gets to be a little contagious - it's a great place to practice and a great community to live in."

to an academic center. "A lot of the cancer that I see has a good chance of cure. The advances in medical oncology are very exciting, every month there is something new for lung cancer, or pancreatic cancer, brain tumors… things are really moving at breakneck speed….people are living longer and better and turning some cancers into chronic diseases."

Seacoast Center Cancer patients also have the advantage of enrolling in clinical trials. According to Erica Tauriello, Manager of the Human Research Program, 36 clinical trials are currently enrolling patents in the cancer center and its affiliates with approximately 60 patients participating in these trials. "Clinical trials are offered for a variety of cancers, including hematologic, cervical, ovarian, prostate, lung, head and neck, and spine and brain metastases. The focus of

Chapter 21: Regardless of "Purse"

As early as 1907, the charitable mission of Wentworth Hospital hit a hard wall of reality when the Board of Trustees reported the amount paid by "paying patients per day of $1.50 was actually $1.07 less than the cost to care for patients that year." Patients paid their bills in cash, some bartered chickens and vegetables, some swept halls as they recuperated, and another group did not pay - whether they could afford it or not. The hospital stayed in business because the deficit was remedied by the generosity of Dover's citizens who, whether they knew it or not, did their part to keep the hospital's lights on, the furnace working, and patients getting care.

The charitable mission and its challenges consumed the hospital's Board of Trustees and became part of Superintendent Grace Haskell's daily drama of saving lives, healing the sick, and paying the bills. Her annual messages were carefully crafted, quickly made her points on selected topics, and charged the Board and the city to help her solve a problem, find the money for a second telephone, a new typewriter, or an electric elevator. She wisely praised her medical staff that needed her as much as she needed them to run the hospital. In 1909 she focused on a dilemma faced by hospital administrators from her time to the present - covering the cost of those

who do not pay or do not fully pay for care. She wrote, "We have performed more free work than any previous year. We have a free bed donated by the Pacific Mills, Cocheco department, for the benefit of its employees, and we trust this bed is but one of the many to be established in the near future."

The Board shared the burden of balancing budgets as they asked taxpayers to make up the deficits through an annual allotment in the city's budget. Yet, the mission of the hospital strengthened even as dependency on city coffers grew. "This fact," the Board reported, "in conjunction with the number of patients treated wholly free, marks a concession in favor of those of limited means and emphasizes the humanitarian purpose toward which the city councils so wisely contribute."

Administrator Mary Callahan, RN

Medical insurance took decades to develop and was not widely accessible until employer paid health insurance became a popular recruiting tool for businesses competing for workers after World War II. The first reference in a WDH annual report came in 1945 with the mention of "Blue Cross and other hospital insurance" by Administrator Mary Callahan, RN, who lamented that the difficulties of running a deficit in order to maintain the hospital and care for patients came without "large endowments to fall back upon." She noted many patients "carry

Blue Cross or hospital insurance" but those who did not also felt no compunction to pay their hospital bills. She said, "It is a bit ironical that we try to show consideration for sick people who in turn do not try to pay bills when they are well."

That year the mayor focused his remarks on the specific cost of running the hospital on the Dover taxpayer noting "the income from all endowments and from the current revenues from patients is far below the actual cost of operation." The deficit that year was $10,000 more than the appropriation of $25,000 which represented $2.00 on the tax rate. He wrote, "We residents of Dover must become hospital-conscious. We must put our shoulders to the wheels and raise a substantial endowment from private sources in order that the annual deficit at the hospital can be lifted, at least in some degree, from the taxpayers."

Concerns with costs and efforts to reduce the hospital's dependence on the city while seeking to expand the size of the hospital led to a fundraising effort in 1947, titled, the *Dover Hospital Campaign Fund*. The hospital needed attention after so many years without substantial improvements. Designs for new spaces were laid out in a carefully crafted promotional brochure, printed in red and black headlined as, "A Plan for Health, Hope and Happiness." The building schematic showed two small additions to the patient pavilions and a large four-story building on the north side of hospital grounds that included an ambulance entrance at the northeast corner. The annual report indicated the campaign raised $172,560, far short of its goal of $500,000. The project was never completed although the location of the hospital's

A PLAN FOR HEALTH, HOPE AND HAPPINESS

The new Dover Hospital has been designed to fill the needs of Dover and nearby Communities. This new modern building is a necessity for every local family.

Think carefully when a neighbor gives you the chance to help. Consider what improved, adequate hospital facilities will mean to you and yours. Then give seriously!

Many families have hospital insurance. But what good is insurance without hospital beds available?

Remember that this is not an annual campaign. It is a one-time appeal that probably will not be repeated in your lifetime. Give accordingly!

Arrange to use the 10-quarterly payment plan. Make four equal payments in 1947, four in 1948 and two in 1949. Give generously!

Think what your investment in the new Dover Hospital will buy — for years to come. It will buy a hospital with enough beds so that you and your family can be cared for IF you need it and WHEN you need it. That's an investment that is worth while.

YOUR INVESTMENT IS NEEDED
Dover Hospital Fund

current Emergency Department, a move that took place in 1986, is in the same location as shown on the schematic in the "Plan for Health, Hope and Happiness."

While funds were inadequate to build the planned addition, they did help support the construction of a smaller project at the back of the Administration Building, parallel to Central Avenue. Project costs were covered by Hill-Burton funds, and a bond floated by the city. According to a *History of the Wentworth-Douglass Hospital* written by Public Relations Director Mary Perry, "What is now known as the '54 addition was built at a total cost in excess of $650,000." The name of the hospital was subsequently changed to Wentworth-Dover City Hospital.

In his earliest annual reports to the city, Vincent DeNobile focused on squeezing out expenses and becoming financially independent. In 1959 he wrote, "Wentworth-Dover City Hospital, more than most others, needs a healthy and stable Operating Fund. The hospital should not continue to lean on the City Treasury to make up the deficit." The next year he made a promise to "break even" and fulfilled the promise in 1963, the last year the city appropriated funds to cover operating expenses.

Each era of reform presented its own pressures to reduce costs, improve quality, adapt processes (i.e. inpatient to outpatient care settings), and inspire innovation through new technology. The implementation in the mid-sixties of Medicare and Medicaid to pay for health care for the elderly and poor led to a period of soaring hospital growth for close

to twenty years. Seeking a way to curb overuse and cut rising costs, Medicare introduced a prospective payment system based on Diagnostic Related Groups in 1983. This inpatient payment method has continually failed to pay for the cost of care resulting in cost shifting to commercial payers and restructuring care to the outpatient arena. In response, managed care and health maintenance organizations (HMOs) flourished in the eighties focusing on prevention, wellness, tight admission controls, and building relationships with other hospitals and health systems.

In the nineties, with the advent of capitation and assumed risk, managed care systems gained a lot of power. CFO Peter Walcek recalled how the HMOs "put a lot of pressure on patients. Unless you got permission to do something or followed the rules that you had to be out of the hospital at a certain time, you were not covered. The pendulum swung too far and employers and employees said it was not working. The marketplace has evolved since then." Walcek also mentioned attempts by the Clinton administration to bring in universal health coverage. "We also had the Clinton Health Plan mixed into the mid-nineties that never saw the light of day, but some of its tenets moved into the private sector where insurers initiated more value-based, outcomes-based business models."

The steadfast effort to make health care affordable over the past century, led by earnest hospital administrators, politicians, and government agencies, continues to be deluged by amazing and costly technological advances, cancer targeting drugs, and new surgical systems supported by legions of info techs and coding experts. President Walker described health care today as "incredibly expensive." He noted, "The cost of pharmaceuticals is going through the roof, biologics and chemotherapy, plus huge increases in generic drug costs and new technology. If you want to buy a new linear accelerator it's $3 or $4 million. Patients want new drugs, new technology to provide the best care, so in order to provide that, the cost equation goes up."

Containing these escalating costs of health care, Walker explained, is "about being creative and trying to look where the future's going." Volume driven systems will change to value driven systems where patient care spreads outside the walls of the hospital to primary care, community health initiatives, and innovative partnerships. Walker said the health system is working on efficiencies where possible, eliminating duplication and making sure patients are on the appropriate protocols. He used the example of back pain treatment. "For patients with low back pain, we are no longer doing MRIs for the first six to eight weeks, depending on the patient's symptoms. It's proven that 80 to 90 percent of patients get better with conservative treatment."

Wentworth-Douglass is part of Granite Health, one of five health systems in NH working on Medicare demonstration projects to reduce costs for Medicare beneficiaries. "We've been able to reduce the cost of care and demonstrate for Medicare that we're improving outcomes," Walker explained. In a more innovative approach to cost-containment, Granite Health developed the Tufts Health Freedom Plan, a suite of tiered and non-tiered commercial plans for New Hampshire, that offers small and large businesses a new and local option to access high quality, cost-effective health care. Other insurers are also taking notice of the hospital's efforts to keep costs reasonable while continuing to provide "best outcomes." Walker said, "That's why they like to do business here. We have the breadth of services they are looking for with a tight focus on quality and cost."

Chapter 22: Good Things Happen - Philanthropy Matters

The history of Wentworth-Douglass began with a single gift. The $100,000 bequest from the estate of philanthropist Arioch Wentworth was the first in a lengthy list of generous donors who believed in the values, goals, and hopes of a hospital in Dover. The Rollins donation built a nurses home, the Douglass donation built a three-story addition replacing the original hospital, and the Dunaway Foundation's generosity supported two wings to create that era's modern hospital. Since the beginning, individuals donated flowers, apples, candy, and newspapers. Many made donations of small sums in gratitude for the extraordinary care of a loved one. Local businesses that understood the value of sustaining a quality health care system for their community contributed larger sums.

While the first recorded campaign in 1947 failed to reach its goal, it did raise close to $200,000 that helped support the construction of the '54 building. The next community-wide fundraiser began in 1984 in response to the NH CON review board's request that the hospital raise $500,000 toward the new construction project. Thanks to the leadership of local businessman, James Kageleiry, the amount raised exceeded the request and came in close to $1 million including generous donations from WDH employees to build a heliport.

Campaign Chairman James Kageleiry (center) accepts a donation from the Janetos family.
(l-r) Paul Janetos, Andrew Janetos, Kageleiry, George Janetos and Lewis Janetos

A 1993 legacy gift, valued at over $1 million from the estate of George E. Morgan, MD, one of the hospital's first surgeons, provided the building blocks for a more formal philanthropy program that began in 2004 with the creation of the Wentworth-Douglass Hospital & Health Foundation (the Foundation). Since its beginning, the Foundation has steadily increased its annual funds raised to support the programmatic and service needs of Wentworth-Douglass Hospital. In 2015, the Foundation raised close to $1.3 million to make a difference in the lives of patients and community members. Donor support of Care-Vans provided 14,100 free rides to and from hospital appointments, Wentworth-Douglass Dental Community Dental Center was able to discount dental services to over 3,000 adults and children, and 1,700 integrative therapy treatments such as Reiki, therapeutic massage, and acupuncture were provided free of charge to patients, helping to reduce stress and ease pain. The Foundation also made a difference for children by supporting programs for therapeutic horseback riding, dance, music and art therapy, and Camp Meridian's unique experience for children with heart defects.

The Foundation met its goal to raise funds for the Garrison Wing project, led by a $250,000 donation from the Hannaford Charitable Foundation for the new addition's Special Care Nursery. This nursery provided small, private rooms where parents can stay with their newborn needing extra care due to premature birth, breathing problems, or dependency on narcotics. Generous community donors and employees named rooms in the new addition and designated areas in the Healing Garden in honor or memory of a loved one.

Simone Believeu, RN and Dir. of Nursing James Mullen, RN top the scale for employee donatio

Hospital President Gregory Walker described the Foundation as the hospital's "future" and a way for people, grateful for the the care of a loved one, to "continue someone's legacy." Former Chairman of the Foundation and Trustee Ann Torr said the Foundation is needed more than ever in these days of reduced reimbursement and increasing cost "in order to keep state-of-the-art health care for our community." She remarked, "We need to have some help, donations go such a long way." At the 1906 Heritage Society Luncheon in 2015, President Walker told the story of a recent donation.

"In May (2015) a woman walked into our Cancer Center and said she had a donation to drop off. It was from her sister, Peg Kayser of Alton Bay, who had passed away. Peg had been a patient and she was so grateful for the compassionate care she received she wanted to show her appreciation. Inside the envelope was a check for $52,000 from her estate, the largest single gift the Cancer Center has ever received. The staff at the Cancer Center was taken completely by surprise; for four years Peg had shared her passions for gardening, her golden retrievers, and many other causes. Peg was a lovely woman, fondly remembered by many. No one knew she had made this provision in her will. Looking back, it would have been great if we could have thanked Peg for recognizing her caregivers in such a meaningful way and providing resources to care for the patients to follow her."

Current Foundation Board Chairman Jay O'Neill, President of Federal Savings Bank, grew more interested in the hospital's fundraising program after visiting one of his employees in the old Birth Center. Her small newborn needed special care and could not leave the nursery. To be with her baby, mom and dad crowded into a small nursery with other anxious parents visiting their tiny newborns. Plans were almost complete for the new Women & Children's Center that would soon give parents and their special care babies private spaces to become a family. "I was impressed with the care and understood the need for the expansion. I also thought it was important that someone from the bank be on the Foundation Board," he said. "As I started to get involved, one of the things I realized was just how much the Foundation gives back to the community; it was a perfect fit for what we do at the bank - giving back and making a better place to raise families. The hospital did the same thing."

Foundation Board members
Jay O'Neill and Rick Card

Kelly Clark, VP for Community Relations and Philanthropy, discovered the Foundation when she assumed her new role at WDH in 2014. While the hospital has endeavored to raise money since its inception in 1906, Ms. Clark believes there is a difference in that effort today. "In the past, philanthropy was not something the hospital had to rely upon to remain healthy and vibrant as an institution; that may not be the case going forward given all the changes in health care external to the hospital. The Foundation Board is going to have a role that is far more important than it had in the first 12 years of its history."

The emotional impact of the Foundation's work was revealed recently at a Healing Garden tour. Several donors had contributed to pavers, trees, and benches for the Healing Garden in the previous two years, but the plaques and engraved pavers were only recently installed. Ms. Clark remarked, "I watched people crying as they found a stone with the name of a loved one, it was very moving. An employee, who donated a plaque in memory of her mother said she sits on a bench now, opposite the paver and has lunch with her mother. I was so touched."

Each gift has its own story and finds a place to benefit others. Richard and Janet Conley of Dover donated $25,000 toward new diagnostic equipment in 2014 because they wanted to see technology used to make a difference. "We like to donate to something that has an actual good outcome like cardiac cath (catheterization) and we are impressed with the staff and pleased Wentworth-Douglass is investing in this type of equipment." Retired UNH professor Bob Adams honored his beloved wife Patricia Adams, MD, creating an endowment in her name with proceeds targeted to programs that "will enhance the quality of life of children, particularly those with special needs."

Durham couple Jackie Eastwood and Mike McClurken donated $75,000 to name the Eastwood Auditorium in the Garrison Wing Conference Center to create a place open to the community for meetings and special events. Their gift was in gratitude for the care they and their employees received at WDH over the years. Bob and Trish DeColfmacker named one of four conference room in gratitude for their life-long connections to the hospital. D. F. Richard Energy and Federal Savings Bank named conference rooms. Funds to name a fourth room were donated by Roger Dionne, an Environmental Services employee who just wanted to "give back" to the hospital he has worked at for close to 30 years. Other local companies, such as Albany International and Measured Progress, generously support the health system that provides care and services for their employees.

Former nurse and Dover resident Nancy Reynolds Boyle named Wentworth-Douglass Hospital as one of the recipients of a trust in her will because the "hospital has always been part of my life," she explained. "I had my tonsils out in 1940 and my appendix out in 1948. I'd been thinking about it for some time. Wentworth-Douglass Hospital is part of my family history and hopefully wise people will know what to do with the money once I'm gone."

While funds frequently support patient care services, donations toward scholarships give employees the chance to begin or continue their education as the caregivers of tomorrow. Over a hundred employees have received scholarships and expanded their roles caring for patients at Wentworth-Douglass. CNO Sheila Woolley said, "These scholarships truly make the difference for an employee struggling to finance their education while taking care of their family's needs. We are so grateful to the donors for supporting this amazing program."

Chapter 23: Auxiliary & Volunteers

The Women's Service Council, precursor to the WDH Auxiliary, began in 1953 with the support of Edna Walck, MD. The Service Council opened a snack bar, run by volunteers, with food donated by community members. Dr. Walck was a general practitioner and the first female physician to join the medical staff in 1933. She eventually limited her practice to administering anesthesia until she retired. She considered it both "a privilege and an obligation" for individuals to become involved in community service. In 1973, with the growth of male participation in hospital volunteer work and for better identification, the Women's Service Council changed its name to Wentworth-Douglass Hospital Auxiliary. Since its founding, the Auxiliary raised over $1,643,000 from a host of fundraisers including dinner theaters, house tours, hospital balls, and proceeds from the Gift Shop to support patient care services at WDH. The Auxiliary's donation of $75,000 to fund the Garrison Wing Healing Garden was the largest single donation when the project began. Auxiliary President Roni Morse said at the time, "We've made many large contributions to the hospital over the years to purchase equipment and support expansion projects. This will be another opportunity to support the hospital, the community, and the employees."

In 2014, the WDH Auxiliary, recognizing the Foundation's strength in fundraising, dissolved their organizational structure and donated their remaining funds to the Foundation to carry on selected projects and their scholarship program for high school students pursuing health care careers through the WDH Auxiliary Endowment Fund. Proceeds from the hospital's Gift Shop, managed by former Auxiliary President Donna Soares and staffed by volunteers, continue to fund the Auxiliary's key initiatives.

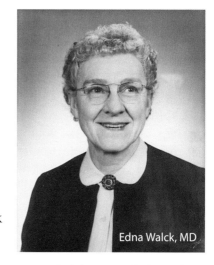
Edna Walck, MD

Volunteer Program

Hospital volunteerism took many forms over Wentworth-Douglass Hospital's history. Initially, external groups and clubs provided goods and services at no charge, as reflected in the 1920 annual report of the city. Ms. Haskell gave thanks for the "Philanthropy Department of the Dover Woman's Club, the History Department of the Dover Woman's Club, Dover Woman's Suffrage Club, and the Hospital Club." The Hospital Club donated money and made articles for the hospital including "slings, bibs, and decorated jars to be used as flower vases."

Hospital Director Vince DeNobile referenced a "new and expanded volunteer program" in his annual report message in 1960 with 30 volunteers donating 2,967 hours. One of those volunteers, Ann Herlihy, continues to donate her time several days a week with a personal accumulation of close to 28,000 volunteer hours from 48 years of volunteer work at WDH.

Volunteer Beryle Banks, former pediatric nurse, remembered a time when volunteers brought in food for the coffee shop originally located in the Douglass building. "I had been volunteering and bringing food into the coffee shop. Dottie Lord brought in chowder on Fridays and everybody knew that. Different organizations took turns doing it." Her first volunteer position was on gift cart duty, a job she cherished because she enjoyed "being out with people." The gift/candy cart retired a few years ago, but Beryle is still active. She's added patient representative and "cuddler" to her volunteer resume. Her cuddling job depends "on what's going on in the nursery" and she is often asked to comfort the dependent babies of drug addicted moms. "I tell the mom I am just here to help out, hold her baby if she is tired or the baby is fussy. My field of nursing was infants and toddlers and I just love kids. I enjoy doing this. It makes me feel good and they appreciate it."

Another volunteer role is part of a unique program that began in 2013, the Patient and Family Advisory Council, under the direction of Mary Krans, Director of Patient Experience. The Advisory Council collaborates with leadership and staff to be the "voice" of patients. Council member Kathy Oby of Barrington said, in an interview in the Spring 2014 *Windows* magazine, she enjoyed the opportunity to give feedback on initiatives and protocols regarding patients. She noted, "Offering our suggestions and seeing some of them come to fruition is an amazing experience." Council member John Barbour said he enjoyed how employees came back and showed the advisors how they made improvements due to Council suggestions. "I can sit back and bark at it, or I can be a part of it," he explained.

Auxilians Donna Soares and Roni Morse

2007 Auxiliary Board

Chapter 24: Stretching the Boundaries

Wentworth-Douglass Hospital officially became part of larger system of care in 2012 with the formation of the Wentworth-Douglass Health System. As the Wentworth-Douglass Foundation grew, the entity became a distinct part of the Wentworth-Douglass Health System along with The Works and Wentworth Health Partners. A recent system joint venture with local physician investors formed the Wentworth Surgical Center in Somersworth as a cost-effective alternative to hospital surgery for low-risk cases.

Relationships flourished with other healthcare partners. As President Walker described, the relationships are "vital to caring for patients seeking the best possible health care" in an era where quality matters even as cost cutting pressures penetrate every program. "I think our relationships with clinical partners are incredibly important. We're being held accountable now for providing care across the continuum, not just within the walls of the hospital, so we need to have strong relationships with home health and hospice that allows us to have influence on the quality of care and how care is handled across a broad outpatient arena."

Walker emphasized the impact of key affiliations with Children's Hospital at Dartmouth and Massachusetts General Hospital. He noted, "It's really important to have relationships with quaternary and tertiary hospitals so patients get the best, most timely care available; we can get on the same protocols over time so we can eliminate duplication of testing - that's what patients want."

Massachusetts General Hospital brings expertise to Wentworth-Douglass community

World-renowned physicians and specialists from Massachusetts General Hospital come to Dover, several days a week, to provide clinical care at the Chest Clinic and the Program for Cancer Genetics, and perform intricate gynecology-oncology, thoracic and lung surgeries. Mass General physicians also work with Wentworth-Douglass physicians on joint program development. Dr. John Schorge has led the Gynecology-Oncology Program since 2008 and Dr. James Allan heads the Thoracic Surgery Program. The hospital's advances in stroke care – in collaboration with Mass General – earned it the Gold Award from the American Heart Association and certification as a Primary Stroke Center from The Joint Commission in collaboration with the American Heart Association/American Stroke Association. This was the result of an effort to excel at stroke care, saving brain tissue, saving lives. In 2012, Dr. Paul Cass remarked the hospital's designation happens to "only a small number of hospitals across this nation."

In July 2012, Wentworth-Douglass and Mass General jointly hired Dr. Peter Hedberg as the trauma medical director for the Wentworth-Douglass Health System. He serves as a full-time acute care and trauma surgeon and provides coverage one weekend per month at Mass General.

As the relationship grew between Mass General and Wentworth-Douglass, clinical affiliations expanded as well. In the summer 2013 Mass General identified Wentworth-Douglass as the "Primary Clinical Affiliate of Massachusetts General Hospital on the New Hampshire Seacoast." Collaborative initiatives focused on expanding relationships in the areas of oncology, cardiovascular, neurosciences, and digestive health.

On April 28, 2016, in a communication to patients and community members, the Boards of Wentworth-Douglass Health System and Massachusetts General Hospital announced they signed a "letter of intent for Wentworth-Douglass Hospital to become a member of the Mass General family and part of the Partners HealthCare System." This agreement was the first formal step in the process to make Mass General the parent organization of Wentworth-Douglass Hospital.

Roger Hamel, chairman of the Wentworth-Douglass Health System Board of Directors said, "Becoming part of the Mass General family will advance our mission to partner with individuals and families to attain their highest level of health and promote the vision for Wentworth-Douglass to be the 'Regional Hub' for health care services in the Seacoast region."

Under terms of the proposed acquisition, Wentworth-Douglass Hospital will keep its name and remain an independently licensed, not-for-profit, charitable health care organization. While becoming part of the Mass General family, Wentworth-Douglass will maintain its own board of trustees, medical staff, community connections and fundraising

activities. Assuming satisfactory completion of due diligence, the negotiation of definitive transaction documents, and appropriate regulatory reviews, the proposed acquisition would take effect by the end of 2016 or early 2017.

Peter L. Slavin, MD, Mass General President expressed his support of the strengthening relationship between the institutions. "Wentworth-Douglass is an institution with strong leadership and a clinical staff committed to delivering care to patients, families and the community. We look forward to working closely with the hospital board, leaders and staff to build upon that solid foundation of exceptional care."

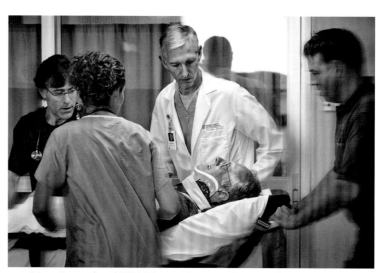

Mass General and WDH Trauma Surgeon Peter Hedberg, MD joins WDH ER Medical Director Lukas Kolm to care for injured patient.

Chapter 25: Caring for Patients

For 110 years the hospital at the top of Garrison Hill has been open all day, all night. Thousands of people worked, learned, prayed, cried, laughed, and cared for their neighbors, friends, and people they never met before. Walls went up, came down, and went up again, but as Robbie Robinson said at the 1986 dedication, "The heart of a hospital is not a building. The heart of a hospital is the hearts and hands of those who work in it and for it… as they carry on their comforting work." If Grace Haskell's "Record of Help" had continued through the years it would be a hefty volume or two or three. Every single person in its history left an imprint.

The caring work of this hospital has changed dramatically, yet in some ways, not at all. CNO Sheila Woolley remarked on the differences in patient care today - the regulatory arena, the quality measures, the documentation, HIPAA, ICD-10, insurance restrictions, cost constraints, new roles as health coaches and navigators, and dealing with "trage-dies" like the heroin addiction and behavioral health issues. Even though technology is rapidly increasing, "the role of the nurse as communicator, caregiver, confidant - none of those pieces have changed."

Medical Staff President Dr. John Novello said "At this hospital there has always been a close relationship between physicians, always congenial and working as a team. I don't think that has changed. The other point…one thing that really distinguishes Wentworth-Douglass now is that they try to be

the best; Greg Walker brought that dimension to the hospital. We went from trying to do good and be a friendly community hospital to a friendly community hospital where we try to become the best at what we do…that kind of mentality, that kind of objective has shaped everything that has happened subsequently and it has all been for the better."

Dr. Cass believes the breadth and depth of the medical staff has increased the sophistication of medical care available at WDH. What is so different? The medical staff is over 400 in number representing specialties and subspecialties - services that just didn't exist years ago. "If you think about Babu Ramdev and Peter Bradley in that little ER…so much has changed. We probably have 40 or 45 programs for the community and the facility itself are all significant changes. Wentworth Douglass today is a regional community hospital that provides basic care and a lot of subspecialty and regional care - very different from when I came here. We were just a sleepy little community hospital."

In January 2016, Wentworth-Douglass received Health-Grades Clinical Excellence Award, recognizing superior clinical quality and patient outcomes across a broad spectrum of services. Only the top five percent of hospitals in the nation earn this award each year. Wentworth-Douglass also received five-star ratings from HealthGrades for Patient Experience, Women's Health, Pulmonary Care, and the treatments of heart failure, respiratory failure, stroke, sepsis, COPD and pneumonia.

Dover Economist Brian Gottlob recently noted the value of a high quality hospital in fueling the local economy. In a *Foster's* news story published in April 2016, he asked, "What's it like when a region doesn't have a hospital? It's much less attractive and has an economic impact by reducing property values." His comments were reinforced by Donna Rinaldi, finance manager at the Greater Dover Chamber of Commerce and member of the Wentworth-Douglass Health System Board of Directors, regarding the impact the hospital has on prospective residents' decisions. She said, "About 50 percent or more of them say they were drawn here because they know there's an award-winning hospital in the area."

Wentworth-Douglass continues into the 21st century with a growing patient base that comes for care from as many as 60 communities. President Walker hopes that 110 years from now "when people look back they'll see as much of a transformation and growth as the past 110 years has been."

Epilogue – August 30, 2016

A warm breeze ruffled a lazy patch of day lilies planted around the base of Wentworth-Douglass Hospital's north side sign. As the gentle wind swirled, the image of a horse drawn buggy emerged; its outline shimmering in the sun. The faint figure of a woman, wrapped in a gossamer shawl, stepped down from the carriage with slow-motion care, the shadow of her shoes barely touching the surface below. A sheer, wide-brimmed bonnet obscured her face, although pale wisps of hair still managed to escape. Caught in a lovely web of illusion, Grace seemed content to go unnoticed.

At first she wasn't sure this was the same place where she served so long as superintendent. The sprawling buildings, just beyond the hospital's sign lacked the flourishes and lovely fresh-air porches she remembered and loved. The welcome clatter of buggies and breathy snort of horses were long gone memories as well. Just looking at the Avenue's dense traffic and the cluster of homes nearby, meant the city had grown rapidly, replacing elegance with noise and clutter. The hospital's name had changed too, probably from a wealthy family's donation or a charitable industrialist. Grace was glad the stone wall along the Avenue was still there although somewhat longer, yet, she admitted, it was in good repair. The Wentworth Home to her left had not changed at all; it was comforting to see it was still a home for the aged. She often considered moving in there herself but the hospital's Board regularly refused her requests to resign. She finally decided to just live on in her superintendent's suite; where she enjoyed

quiet evenings watching the sun melt slowly into the farmland across the Avenue.

It was near noon as she moved down the busy road. Groups of employees were seated outside at wooden tables under dark green umbrellas eating lunch and enjoying a break in their day. Some were tapping on palm-size objects or bringing them to their ears and talking as if they were some kind of telephone. One group used the miniature machine to take a picture that showed up instantly in a little frame. Music played from another one. Grace shook her head at this amazing invention and wondered how the clunky contraptions of her era - telephones, cameras, typewriters, and record players - could ever fit inside a thing so small. She hoped they paid as much attention to their patients as they did to those devices.

All of these young people had badges on, probably with their names and jobs titles, but even with her old spectacles Grace could not read the fine print. She did question their choice in attire. Most wore pajama-like cotton pants and tops in an array of colors. It was so hard to tell who were nurses, or doctors, lab workers, radiology techs, or housekeepers. A little starch and a swift pass of a firm iron would do wonders to get rid of the ruts and wrinkles they seemed to be ignoring. In her day, crisp white uniforms were required for women and doctors proudly wore dark suits, stiff shirts, and broad ties. She passed a woman in a pretty dress wearing sandals; her toes were painted a bright turquoise. Her legs were bare. Oh, my, whatever happened to sturdy pumps and silk stockings? Another man wore a plaid shirt with sleeves rolled up and a bright tie. Maybe he was a doctor or maybe doctors ate somewhere else. She shook her head again.

A trio of ambulances rushed past the patio, lights blinking, sirens blaring. It must be a terrible accident. Grace watched the ambulance drivers unload a young man, writhing in pain, onto a mobile bed. She slipped inside the Emergency Department as they wheeled the hurting patient into a treatment room. A team of men and women, dressed in those cotton outfits, rushed to help as a man in a white coat seemed to direct the action, maybe he was a doctor. They all washed their hands then put on thin rubber-like gloves as they attached long cords to the patient that led to a wall of blinking machines. They seem to really value cleanliness. More infections might have been prevented in the hospital's early years if they had thought of this strict attention to detail. The team certainly seemed to know what to do. Someone pulled out one of those hand held objects and used it to call for a surgeon and told the OR to get ready for the trauma victims. What a timesaver.

The wall-mounted boxes, with smaller versions on wheels, made odd beeping sounds as numbers flashed on and off. She thought she saw blood pressure measurements and they didn't look good. The patient had lost a lot of blood. They injected a pain medication as they cut off his clothes to reveal a nasty compound fracture. Even though she was a nurse, she winced at the site of an open wound. She even felt that same sense of dread when accident victims had come into her hospital so long ago. Her training always gave her confidence to know what to do and she sensed this team was highly skilled. Saving this young man's life was all

ARIOCH WENTWORTH
FOUNDER OF THE WENTWORTH HOSPITAL
BORN JUNE 13, 1813   DIED MARCH 12, 1903
GIFT OF WILLIAM HALL WENTWORTH

that mattered at the moment. She hoped the current superintendent would commend this team for doing such a fine job.

She left them to their work, passing through a waiting room with anxious family members into a long, carpeted hallway. A sign for the Seacoast Cancer Center marked a doorway on her left. How impressed she was that the hospital had such a large space to take care of cancer patients. When the door opened she heard someone playing a guitar. She peeked in to see a musician at the end of a hall playing and smiling for everyone who passed by; it was so soothing she almost stopped to enter but moved on instead. She arrived in a spacious area with a fireplace flickering inside a stone wall. A fire in August? How wasteful. It did seem cool inside the hospital, even near the fireplace, in fact, it was very pleasant and not a fan in sight. The glint of a wide, gold-framed portrait caught her eye and she knew immediately who lived on in that canvas, Arioch Wentworth. Although much older than Grace, Mr. Wentworth's portrait seemed as fresh as the day it was hung in her Administration Building.

She moved closer to the sliding entrance doors, centered in a wall of windows. While lovely and bright, her first concern was more about the practicality of the space and how much work it was to just keep all those windows clean. The sound of a waterfall interrupted her thoughts as she turned to see water streaming over an enormous granite wall; it looked a lot like a map of New Hampshire. What a clever idea. The café to its left was a busy place. A lovely woman was dishing out soup into cardboard bowls and filling paper cups with coffee. As more people, wearing those somewhat wrinkly yet, she had

to admit, practical cotton togs, cued up for their meals, a tall man in a dark suit asked for a cup of tea. A co-worker called him Greg and wished him a good morning. Maybe he was a doctor. He did look like he was in charge of something. For a moment he turned to look at her; she even thought he could sense her presence. The moment passed. He went on his way.

She noticed the sign for Starbucks listing coffee choices and prices. She did love a good cup of Maxwell House coffee; remembering it really was *good to the last drop*. She wasn't sure what a Caramel Macchiato was, but its price of $3.50 was more than a one day stay at the Wentworth Hospital in the last century. Oh, how things had changed.

She passed a charming gift shop and turned left. As she entered the next hall Grace was greeted by a sign declaring the Garrison Wing, as "a place of education and healing." She was so impressed with the epithet's meaning, she almost missed the old, sepia photos along the hallway of a time and place she knew so well in Dover - its garrison homes, mills, and downtown businesses. She wandered into the library noticing the sparse collection of medical books. For a hospital this size books should be stacked along all the walls. Instead, long counters were covered with thin boxes attached to flat keyboards. The letters on the keyboards were in the same places as the keys on Grace's old Corona typewriter. Where does the paper go? She could see the words a young student typed inside the box but she was sure the student could not take the whole machine with her to a class. Confounded for a moment, Grace was about to shake her head again when another machine came to life at the back of the room, spit-

ting pieces of printed paper into a tray on the top. Ah, that's where it was.

The elevator doors opened outside the library and Grace stepped in. The fourth floor was a beautiful space for patients, so quiet, so big, look at those windows. She reminded herself washing windows was not her problem anymore. She joined a small group of people as they asked a very ill patient if they could come in for rounds. Each member of the group introduced themselves - one was a pharmacist, another a social worker. A young man said he was a nurse and a young woman was a doctor. Oh, my, how roles had changed. Grace could only imagine the disruption brought on by a male nursing student invading the female sanctity of the old Rollins Nurses Home.

The team asked the frail woman a few questions, she smiled and thanked them for coming. As the others moved on, another nurse came in, adjusted the patient's pillows, smoothed her blankets and held her hand as she fell asleep. Grace wiped a tear. It was good to see some things had not changed.

She passed patient rooms with some kind of hanging picture frame that seemed to contain talking movies in bright colors, a head shaker for sure. Smaller machines on wheels, blipped and beeped to no apparent rhythm. Visitors dabbed incessantly at those small, hand-held devices making Grace wonder what happened to conversation even though she had seen their value in the emergency room.

The Women & Children's center was her next stop. She never

had children of her own but she loved babies and hoped to see some today. She eased through locked doors without anyone the wiser - it was fun to be so invisible. She joined a mother in labor. She knew the sounds - the grunts, groans and screams that varied from one mother to another. It was time to push. A small warm bed waited for the newborn in this grand room filled with quite an entourage - the father, at least she thought he was the father, two nurses, a midwife, another older woman she guessed was the mother's mother - they all seemed to be staying. How unusual and where was the doctor? The mother pushed and everyone pushed, even Grace felt the need. The baby's head slid out, a crown of fuzzy dark hair. The shoulders wriggled out with the next big push, then the rest of him. Grace shouted, "It's a boy!" Of course, no one heard her. They were all crying and laughing and hugging each other - mother, father, grandmother, even Grace was swept up with joy. While it had become a little more of a team sport, it seemed birthing hadn't changed at all.

Sure the hospital was bigger with more stuff and things that beeped, blipped, and sometime blared. The ambulances were gone now. An injured young man was resting comfortably after surgery and a new little boy found his powerful voice in a room in a hospital in Dover. Grace had hated to leave the hospital so long ago but her time was up then and it was over again. She was pleased to find the hospital running smoothly and content to let it go for now. Her ride was looming outside in a beautiful garden. She knew it was the place where her nurses' home had once stood - its time had come and gone as well. That warm breeze was back, weaving through the garden's tall grasses, touching the leafy tendrils of an elegant sculpture; as it moved, she slowly faded away.

Acknowledgements

My deepest gratitude to everyone who supported this history project. First, to the people I never knew: Arioch Wentworth, Dover Mayors, Aldermen and Councilors, and Grace P. Haskell. My thanks to Mr. Wentworth who funded the Dover hospital, the city's resolute support of Wentworth's legacy and Grace's 30 years of leadership, instilling the core values that remain in effect today - caring, teamwork, excellence, integrity and respect.

Thank you to everyone I interviewed for their openness and enthusiasm about the hospital's past, present and future. Thank you to my readers for their feedback and thoughtful suggestions: to Vivian Pelletier who corrected the errant punctuation and rambling descriptives, to Wes Kennedy who liked the beginning and Pat Kennedy who read it to the end, to Jerry Daley for suggesting I interview Ruth Griffin, to Dawn Fernald and Kelly Clark for their valuable feedback and Sheila Woolley for her grateful and emotional reaction. Thanks to Peter Walcek for finding misplaced numbers and even more, to Daniel Dunn, Mary Krans and Jackie Small for listening to me ramble on along the way, to Bill Irvine for coaching so well and caring so much, to Jeff Hughes for great suggestions, to Ellen Caille for special assistance, and to Ann Torr for reading it all and enjoying the memories. Thanks also to Irene McCain, Sharon Rossitor and Kendra Langus for finding elusive doctors. Kudos to two great editors, Cathy Beaudoin, for her love of commas and historical perspective and Elly Laliberte for her exquisite attention to details and coordination expertise. Thank you to Dan Mulholland for knowing more than most about the hospital's history. Thanks to Rick Hall for working with me on one more print project and to designer Bill Wolff for his artistry and love of history.

A special thanks to Alice Poole for always being there to organize historical chaos and smile through it all, to Greg Walker for asking me to write the history - it was a joy.

To Brian Evans-Jones and the Jewett Writer's Circle for helping me make Grace Haskell real and imaginary at the same time and to Frank Biehl who read this book in its roughest stages and still thought it would work.

Wentworth-Douglass Hospital/Health System Timeline

1900 13,207 Dover population

1904   City Council of Dover, NH accepted receipt of
Arioch Wentworth's legacy $100,000 to
build a hospital called the Wentworth

1906   Aug. 29 - New ambulance, white with rubber tires,
could be fitted for one or two horses
Aug. 30 - Wentworth Hospital opens. 30 beds.
75 patients, 5 births (1% of city's births)

1907   Hospital expands to 42 beds

1910 13,247 Dover Population

1910   400 patients, 41 births (12% of city's births)
Additional land purchased purchased from Haley
property for $5,700 (will eventually sell part back to
Rollinsford and later buy land back again)

1914   Dietician added - required to be a registered hospital

1916   Measles epidemic

1917   World War impacts home front, economy and
hospital "Hooverized"

1918   Spanish flu epidemic impacts hospital X-ray
department established
Hospital expands to 50 beds

1919   Hon. Edward W. Rollins donated $25,000 to erect
nurses home, as a memorial to the late Mrs. Gladys
A. Rollins (increased to $81,000)

1920 13,029 Dover Population

1920   950 patients, 128 births (34.88% of city's births)
Nursing shortage comes close to temporarily
closing hospital

1922   Rollins Nurses Home opens
Hospital expands to 75 beds

1925   Wentworth Hospital rated "Class A" with new
equipment and new lab

1926   Motorized ambulance supplanted the
horse-drawn vehicle

1930 13,573 Dover Population

1930   1,109 patients, 127 births

1939   Nursing education program affiliated with Boston
City Hospital for study of communicable disease
and pediatrics

1940 13,990 Dover Population

1940   1,722 patients, 252 births

1940 Nursing education program adds 3 month training in psychiatrics at NH State Hospital

1950 15,874 Dover Population

1950 3,027 admissions
Electrocardiology service established

1952 Nursing school suspended

1953 Women's Service Council formed with support of Dr. Edna Walck

1954 New addition opens with 33 patient beds, 24 bassinets. Features new operating room, obstetrical suite, new kitchen and dining room, x-ray, laboratory, and emergency rooms

1955 Wentworth-Dover City Hospital (new name)
Dover celebrates Centennial
40-hour work week established for nurses

1958 Estate of Louise B. Douglass donates $500,000 for new wing

1960 19,131 Dover Population

1960 4,111 admissions, 537 births
Volunteer program begins

1961 Douglass addition opens

1961 Rollins Nurses Home converted the first floor to medical offices, 2nd floor rooms for Strafford Guidance Center, and basement space for physical therapy

1962 Physical Therapy Department opens - relocates to larger '54 building basement in 1968

1965 Hospital names Paul C. Young, MD, as full-time hospital pathologist

1966 Dunaway Foundation gives Dover Hospital $500,000 for addition

1968 Dunaway Pavilion Opens - adds new pathology department, expanded radiology services, physical therapy and rehabilitation service area, and new emergency rooms.
Hospital expands to 148 beds - includes 4-bed Intensive Care Unit

1970 20,850 Dover Population

1970 7,077 admissions, 709 births
Anna E. Dunaway Memorial Building - extended care facility opens - adding 31 beds for total of 178 beds - last increase in beds

1973 Women's Service Council changes name to Wentworth-Douglass Hospital Auxiliary
WDH implements regional blood bank depot

1976	Six-bed psychiatric unit opens on Douglass 2
1977	New wing opens - features six operating rooms, a central sterilizing room, pharmacy, a nine-bed recovery room, a holding room, laboratory darkroom for X-rays and a new central stores warehouse 5-bed Surgicare unit opens
1978	Hospital buys land from Rollinsford for parking
1979	Oncology program begins, psychiatric unit closed

1980   22,377   Dover Population

1980	7,870 admissions, 938 births
1981	Hospital separates from city WDH designated Level III Trauma Center
1982	WDH Designated Level II Trauma Center
1983	Ultrasound equipment added CON approved for radiation therapy at WDH
1984	Nursery rated Level II
1985	WDH and FMH begin joint venture to purchase mobile mammography van
1986	VP George H.W. Bush dedicated new $23 million wing

1986	WDH opens Care Connection in Durham
1988	Third floor addition to new wing opens - Douglass North
1989	Women's Life Imaging opens fixed unit Marsh Brook Rehab opens in Somersworth - joint venture of WDH & FMH

1990   25,042   Dover Population

1990	7,209 admissions, 917 births 1st laparoscopic gall bladder procedure Video EEG added WDH Child Care Center opens
1991	Laser Lithotripsy performed at WDH to treat kidney stones
1992	2-bed Sleep Disorders Center opens
1993	Renovated Birth Center opens Seacoast Cancer Center opens with both radiation and medical oncology
1994	Neighborhood Free Clinic opens in collaboration with The Clinic WDH acquires Squamscott Visting Nurse and Hospice Care Hospital-owned primary care opens in Durham - Durham Health Center

1995 WDH acquires The Works Athletic Club

1999 Rollins building demolished to make way for
expansion - bricks saved/given to employees
as mementos

2000 26,884 Dover Population

2000 5,239 admissions, 625 births
Care-Van Transport service begins
Integrative Therapy program begins
Parking deck added

2001 Wound Healing Institute opens

2002 Ambulatory Building opens - features Lily Ford
Aquatic Pool, Rehabilitation Department,
Same Day Surgery, Endoscopy Center
Fixed MRI installed

2003 New addition opens - features new lobby, expanded
Seacoast Cancer Center,
Emergency and Imaging Services
Additional parking deck completed

2004 Hospital establishes Wentworth-Douglass
Hospital & Health Foundation
Hospitalist program begins
Seacoast Cancer Center adds high dose
rate bracytherapy

2005 Wentworth-Douglass Community Dental
Center opens
Hyperbaric Oxygen Center opens

2006 Robotic Surgery begins

2007 WDH and Children's Hospital at Dartmouth
collaborate on pediatric specialty medicine
care center at WDH
Ambulatory building opens 3rd floor addition -
features CHaD at WDH, Center for Pain
Management, and 6-bed Sleep Disorders Center
Joint Replacement Center opens on 3 South

2008 Affiliation with Massachusetts General Hospital
augments stroke program, adds GYN oncology
services at WDH
Seacoast Cancer Center adds Novalis TX for
stereotactic radio surgery
Child Life Specialist program begins

2009 WDH opens two Professional Centers -
(1) off of Spaulding Turnpike's Exit 9 in Dover
featuring lab, imaging and medical offices and
(2) on Rt. 125 in Lee, NH, featuring a Walk-In
urgent care center, lab, imaging and medical offices
Chest Clinic opens to treat lung disease/cancer

2010 29,987 Dover Population

2010 8021 admissions, 980 births

2010   Parking garage expansion
Northern New England Spine Center and Center for
Medical Genetics opens
Cardiology adds new interventional lab

2011   Construction begins on 4-story addition

2012   Sleep Disorders Center accredited
WDH first in NH recognized as Primary
Stroke Center

2013   Garrison Wing opens
WDH and Mass General expand affiliation,
name WDH as Primary Clinical Affiliate of
Massachusetts General Hospital on the
New Hampshire Seacoast

2014   Community Benefit dollars targeted for Behavioral
Health Program
Cardiovascular Center adds 3D imaging system
WDH Express Care opens in Dover
Wentworth Surgical Center opens in Somersworth -
a joint venture between WDH and area physicians
for low risk, lower cost surgery

2015   Wentworth Health Partners awarded ambulatory
health care accreditation and primary care medical
home certification from the Joint Commission
Lee walk-in changes name to Express Care
Women & Children's Center sees highest number of
births at 1163

2016   Boards of Wentworth-Douglass Health System and
Massachusetts General Hospital announce plans for
Wentworth-Douglass Hospital to become a member
of the Mass General family and part of the Partners
HealthCare System
Wentworth-Douglass celebrates 110 years

History of WDH Administrators

Grace Haskell, RN - 1906-1937

Katherine Hall, RN - 1937-1944

Averil O. Brown - 1944-45 Acting (Dir. of Nursing Service)

Mary Callahan, RN - 1945 - 1955

John Keene - 1956 (left after a few months to enter Episcopal training school)

Leslie Hoitt - 1956 - 1958 Acting (Dir. of Nursing Service)

Irving Rosenthal - 1958 - 1959

Vince DeNobile - 1959- 1974

Lawrence DesRosier - 1975 - appointed - never served

John Beckwith - 1975 - 1978

Norman Brown - 1978 (April - June) - interim

William Richwagen - 1978 - June 1989

Walter Hersey - 1989 - interim 2 months

Ralph Gabarro - 1989 - 1996

Walter Behn - 1996 - Jan. 1997 - Interim

Gregory Walker - 1997 (Jan) - present

Bibliography

Kearns Goodwin, Doris. *The Bully Pulpit*. Kindle ed. New York, New York: Simon & Schuster.

www.americasbesthistory.com

Annual reports City of Dover New Hampshire, 1904-1980

www.inventors.about.com

www.history.com/topics/1918-flu-pandemic

www.pbs.org/healthcarecrisis/history.htm

Bennet, MD, Roland J. "The First Laboratory of the Wentworth Hospital"

"WDH Remembers Lily Ford and Her 78 Years of Service." *Windows To Your Health* - Winter, 2012

Wentworth Hospital Board of Trustees Meeting Minutes, 1927, 1933

www.eyewitnesstohistory.com/pearl.htm

http://history1900s.about.com/od/timelines/tp/1940timeline.htm

time.com/4083274/ballpoint-pen/ - 0ct. 29, 2015 post

http://history1900s.about.com/od/timelines/tp/1940timeline.htm

http://www.pbs.org/healthcarecrisis/history.htm

"Madeline Kennedy Remembers," *Keeping Pace*, Mar. 20, 1998

https://en.wikipedia.org/wiki/Peyton_Place_(novel)

1950s, *Dover Cookbook & History*, Cathy Beaudion

http://history1900s.about.com/od/timelines/tp/1940timeline.htm

"Dr. Walck Wills $25,000 - Auxiliary Founder," *Newsoscope*, Feb. 1979

www.medicalnewstoday.com

"Jaycees name DeNobile Outstanding Man," *Foster's Daily Democrat*, Mar. 1963

"Hospital Honors DeNobile," *Foster's Daily Democrat*, Apr. 1, 1975

"City Construction Projects from Dunaway trust," *Foster's Daily Democrat*, Aug. 27, 1967

"Anna E. Dunaway Dedicate Wing at Hospital," *Foster's Daily Democrat*, Oct. 12, 1970

"DeNobile Releases Annual Wentworth Hospital Report," *Foster's Daily Democrat*, May 8, 1967

www.CDC.gov

Profiles in science - National Library of Medicine http://profiles.nlm.nih.gov

"Hospital Needs No City Tax Money," *Foster's Daily Democrat*, Jan. 11, 1966

"See Hospital Flying on Own Within One Year," *Foster's Daily Democrat*, Dec. 12, 1963

"Rare Operation Succeeds," *Foster's Daily Democrat*, Feb. 26, 1971

"He wasn't scared until… ," *Foster's Daily Democrat*, Jan. 26, 1976

"The Three Worlds of Dr. Adams," *Foster's Daily Democrat*, Mar. 12, 1973

"High Court Says Hospital Winner," *Foster's Daily Democrat*, Feb. 28, 1974

"Dover Clashes Spark Departure," *Foster's Daily Democrat*, Dec. 31, 1974

"Hospital Starts Addition," *Foster's Daily Democrat*, Oct. 1, 1975

"New Hospital Wing Dedicated Sunday," *Foster's Daily Democrat*, Mar. 3, 1977

"Psychiatric patients integrated at WDH," *Foster's Daily Democrat*, Nov. 5, 1979

"Dinner honors Dr. Galt's 30 years of service," *Foster's Daily Democrat*, Mar. 2, 1977

"Wentworth-Douglass Obtains New Angiography Equipment," *Free Press*, May 31, 1977

"Hospital Opens Surgicare Unit," *Foster's Daily Democrat*, Dec. 8, 1977

"Borning Room Makes Giving Birth New Again," *Foster's Daily Democrat*, Jun. 5, 1978

"The Return of the Midwife," *Foster's Daily Democrat*, Sept. 9, 1975

"Hospital at Dover Plans to Expand Nursing Program," *Manchester Union Leader*, Sept. 29, 1976

"WDH Blessed with Auxilian and Volunteers," *Newsoscope*, January 1978

"Dover Hospital Buys Additional Property," *Foster's Daily Democrat*, Mar. 1, 1978

"Richwagen Named W-D Hospital Head," *Foster's Daily Democrat*, Jun. 16, 1978

"History of Medicine," www.medicalnewstoday.com

"Hospital plans bid for independence," *Foster's Daily Democrat*, Jul. 9, 1980

"Free Wentworth-Douglass," *Foster's Daily Democrat*, Nov. 19, 1980

"A piece of the action (re: independence bid)," *Foster's Daily Democrat*, Mar. 24, 1981

"If trauma threatens, W-D Hospital is set," *Foster's Daily Democrat*, Apr. 17, 1981

"Hospital is separated from city," *Foster's Daily Democrat*, Mar 5, 1982

"Trimmed W-D Proposal given OK," *Foster's Daily Democrat*, Jun. 29, 1984

"Hospital OKs $70g helistop," *Foster's Daily Democrat*, Jul. 10, 1986

"State Favors Two Hospitals Multi Million Dollar Expansion Projects," *Manchester Union Leader*, Jun. 6, 1984

"Nursery Rated Level II," *Newsoscope*, April 1984

"$23m hospital expansion kicked off," *Foster's Daily Democrat*, Nov. 17, 1984

"Two area hospitals sign affiliation agreement," *Foster's Daily Democrat*, Sept. 27, 1985

"Wentworth-Douglass' impressive effort (dedication w/VP Bush)," *Foster's Daily Democrat*, Sept. 8, 1986

"Wentworth-Douglass Fun Run on Sunday," *Foster's Daily Democrat*, May 9, 1984

"Bill recognizes Dover hospital as non-profit," *Foster's Daily Democrat*, May 5, 1988

https://www.google.com/about/company/history

"Maine Man selected as WDH Director," *Foster's Daily Democrat*, Jul. 24, 1989

"Gabarro reflects on first months at WDH," *Foster's Daily Democrat*, Jan. 31, 1990

"Wentworth-Douglass Hospital Offers Newest Form of Gall Bladder 'Surgery,'" *WDH Focus Magazine*, Spring 1991

"Failure of hospitals' merger exposed health care troubles," *Foster's Daily Democrat*, Mar. 19, 1993

"Center at WDH is cancer's newest enemy," *Foster's Daily Democrat*, Nov. 22, 1993

"Wentworth-Douglass Birth Center opens with 5 babies," *Foster's Daily Democrat*, Jun. 30, 1993

"Dover physician retires," *Foster's Daily Democrat*, Jan. 27, 1993

"Dover physician calls end to lengthy career," *Foster's Daily Democrat*, Oct. 16, 1993

"Last of six hospitals signs merger concept," *Foster's Daily Democrat*, Nov. 11, 1994

"Neighborhood Free Clinic story," *Portsmouth Herald*, Mar. 28, 1994

"Hanging up his scalpel (Dr. Temple retires)," *Foster's Daily Democrat*, Aug. 1, 1996

"New Wentworth-Douglass president is a N.J. exec," *Foster's Daily Democrat*, Dec. 20, 1996

"New head of WDH settles in," *Foster's Daily Democrat*, Feb. 3, 1997

"Infants welcomed from the start," *Foster's Daily Democrat*, Feb. 24, 1998

"Decade's top national and international news stories," www.boston.com, 2015

"Project marks the end of a $20m expansion," *Foster's Daily Democrat*, Aug. 9, 2003

"WDH offering new radiation treatment equipment," *Foster's Daily Democrat*, Nov. 23, 2004

"Murder Mystery Dinner Raised over $8,000 for Cardiovascular Interventional Lab," *Windows To Your Health* - Summer 2010 - 2009 Annual Report

"Cardiovascular Care," *Windows To Your Health* - Fall 2012

"Dover Couple Supports Purchase of Advanced Cardiovascular Equipment," *Windows To Your Health* - Spring 2014

"WDH takes Quantum Leap," *Foster's Daily Democrat*, April 2008

https://madeinamericathebook.wordpress.com/2011/09/21/breastfeeding-history

https://www.babyfriendlyusa.org/faqs

"Wentworth-Douglass Hospital Opens Joint Replacement Center," *Windows To Your Health* - Winter 2007

"The Northern New England Spine Center Partnership," *Windows To Your Health* - Summer 2010

A surgical work of art - Wentworth-Douglass adds robotic surgery," *Foster's Daily Democrat*, Jun. 13, 2006

"WDH Auxiliary pledges $75,000 To Support Expansion Project," *Windows to Your Health* - Winter, 2012

"WDH is first in NH Awarded as Primary Stroke Center," *Windows To Your Health* - Fall 2012

"Hospitals help drive Seacoast economy," *Foster's Daily Democrat*, Apr. 17, 2016

"Wentworth-Douglass joins Mass General family," *Foster's Daily Democrat*, Apr. 28, 2016